Never Kiss a

Marilyn Anderson

G000151119

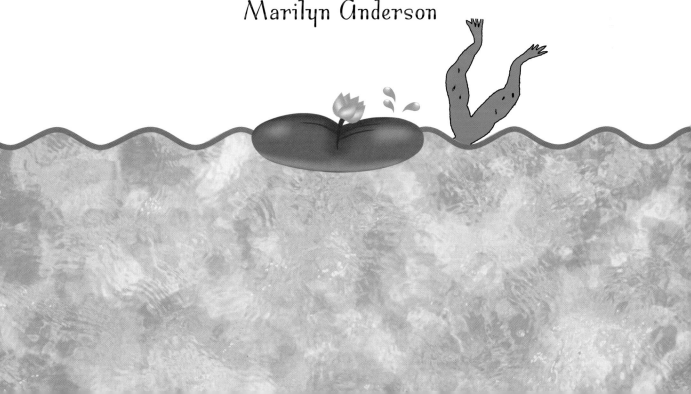

Published by Red Rock Press
New York, New York
U.S.A.

Cover and book design by
Kathleen Herlihy-Paoli,
Inkstone Design.

Cover art: Adapted from a photo by
R.D. Rubic of a mural in Manhattan
Bistro, New York, N.Y.

Interior illustrations by
Marilyn Anderson

Printed in Singapore

Acknowledgments

There are lots of people to thank, including my friends, my family and my frogs. First and foremost, I thank Dennis Lanning for his never-ending inspiration and encouragement, advice and wisdom. And for his wonderful sense of humor, which kept me smiling even when I was in Frog Hell. If ever there was a prince, it's Dennis! Thanks also to Cliff Carle for graciously editing my manuscript. Luckily, I have a lot of fabulous funny friends, who gave fabulous froggy feedback: Dan Beckerman, Sydney Blake, Marvin Braverman, Ira Heffler, Mark Miller and Richard Rossner. Then there are my friends who listened to me talk about frogs incessantly—over and over—and they *still* laughed. And others who egged me on: Wendy Kram, Steve Forest, Karin McKevoy, Felice Peres and Ralph Phillips. Thanks also to David Samson and Susan Schaefer for their knowledge and friendship. Special thanks go to my wonderful parents, Jules and Lenore. Last but not least: Thanks to the frogs! Sure, I may have revealed some of your dark secrets, but don't worry—all names and identifying details have been changed to protect the slimy.

Love to you all,
Marilyn "Frogerella" Anderson

Once Upon a Lily Pad

"*Someday my prince will come.*" What a romantic thought! And like millions of little girls, I grew up believing it. Why? Simple, I loved fairytales—especially the ones where the girl marries the handsome prince. He would slay fiery dragons, fight ruthless witches and outwit despicable relatives just to find the woman he loved. And make her his princess!

I yearned for the day it would happen to me. The only problem was *it didn't*. I waited and waited. My damn prince didn't show!

Then I realized that times had changed. I didn't have to *wait* for my prince. I could go out and *search* for him.

What messed me up then was that silly fairytale, "The Frog Prince." That's the one where a princess sees a frog in the road. He tells her that an evil witch cast a spell on him and, if she kisses him, he'll turn into a prince. At first the princess doesn't believe him. She's no fool. But finally she plants one on his slimy green lips. And *voilà!* He transforms into an absolute hunk of royalty. They fall in love, get married and live happily ever after!

Kiss a frog and he'll turn into a prince. Right! Sure! Who would come up with such a preposterous concept?

Actually, it came from German folklore. But the original storyteller must've been a *guy*—obviously some poor ugly schnook, *i.e., frog*—who wanted to get women to kiss him, i.e., to *sleep* with him. Who knew he'd be affecting women all over the world for centuries?

God knows he affected me. Hey, I was impressionable. So I went after those frogs. I kissed, I puckered and I smooched. But guess what? No princes appeared. I was heartsick. My friends tried to perk me up. "After all," they said, "you have to kiss a lot of frogs before you find your prince."

Then one day, the realization hit me—it's simply not true! Frogs DO NOT turn into princes. Which is not to say they don't turn into anything. To the contrary, after a night of "leapfrog," they frequently turned into rats, snakes or just plain *turkeys*.

Which is why I wrote this book: To warn women to STAY AWAY from frogs!

That's right: Do not waste your precious time (or lips) on a frog. Get rid of him as soon as you detect the first sign of slime or a snippet of ribbet. And tell all your friends: You can't find a prince if you're busy kissing frogs!

The following pages feature an assortment of frogs so that you can easily recognize them and make quick, wart-free getaways.

And what makes me an authority? I've been single *forever*. I've dated the rich and the homeless, the tall and the pygmy, the tan and the albino. I've met frogs on beach towels and ski lifts, in supermarkets and *meat* markets. I've met them on park benches, bench-pressing and one who was pressing his pants. Once, my hairdresser's gynecologist gave my number to a man on a passing gurney! Oh yeah, I've had blind dates and bland dates. The only date I haven't had is a *wedding date.*

Now, I'd like to prevent you from making my mistakes. So please start turning the pages, and remember: *Never Kiss a Frog!*

Table of Contents

Section 1

Gone with the Warts

Section 2

Ribbeting Experiences

Section 3

Frog Family Album

Section 4

Nightmare on Slime Street

Section 5

Close Encounters of the Frog Kind

Section 6

Hoppily Ever After

Gone with the Warts

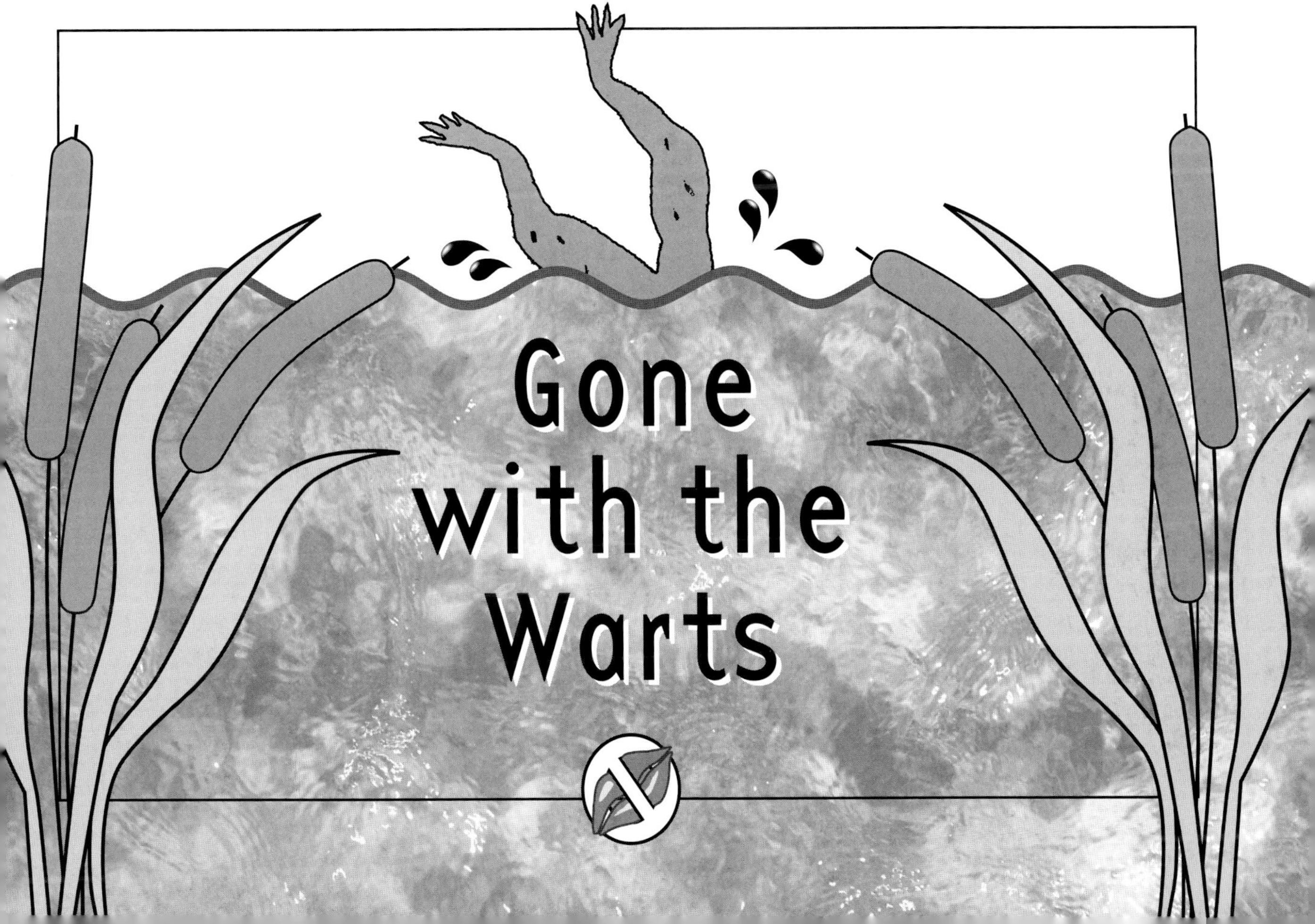

The Long-Term-Go-Nowhere Frog

He's your best friend. Your parents love him. He doesn't *require* sex; he gives you *occasional* sex; he's *always good* for sex. None of this matters. You've dated him practically forever and you're not married.

Get rid of him. *He's a frog!*

Almost every single woman I know has had one of these. Three years, five years, 10 years—it's comfortable. He's always there. Right! He's just never there to say, "I do."

I have known *my* Long-Term-Go-Nowhere Frog —it's embarrassing to tell you this—for 15 years. And when did I suspect it might not go anywhere? Would you believe the first night?

I was at a disco. After sweating up the dance floor with a dozen dull guys, I took a breather and sat at the bar. Suddenly, *he* sat on the barstool next to me. My heart raced. My stomach did flip-flops. Either it was the "thunderbolt" or a massive case of food poisoning. (Actually, it was a massive case of *frog* poisoning.)

He spoke. "Do you come here often?"

I overlooked his froggy line, and—thinking about the past four Fridays I'd stayed until closing—stuttered: "No . . . uh . . . it's my first time."

"I love virgins," he said with a smile. That was it. The bond was forged.

It's not that he was outrageously handsome. Teddy-bearish, I'd say, with short brown hair that matched his tortoiseshell glasses. And in his preppy shirt and baggy pants, he would never make the cover of *GQ*.

But somehow there was this mysterious

Telltale Signs of a Go-Nowhere Frog

1. It's been seven years and you still have separate apartments.

2. You fight like married people, you make up like married people, you're even having as little sex as married people—but you're not married.

3. It's Saturday night and he suggests a romantic evening watching "Wrestlemania."

4. Year in and year out, you keep bringing up the subject of marriage and he keeps saying, "Marriage is for boring, old, regular people. You and me, baby, we're special."

5. Year in and year out, you keep buying it. Which brings me to some critical definitions:

PRINCE

A. The man you are going to marry.

B. The man with whom you will live happily ever after. (Or at least until the divorce.)

FROG

A. Any man you are not going to marry.

B. *Any man you are not going to marry!*

C. ANY MAN YOU ARE NOT GOING TO MARRY!

---

connection. Who knew it was a connection that would stick like glue for years? Sort of like Crazy Glue on my heart. (More like Silly Putty on my brain!)

I asked him to dance. He said no. It seemed he had two left feet. (I should've checked right then and there and seen that they were *webbed* feet.) He shrugged apologetically. "Why don't we talk?"

We went back to his place and talked all

night. It was obvious we were doomed. Sure, our souls matched, and our bodies fit perfectly—but our lifestyles were at opposite ends of the universe.

He gets up at 4:30 in the morning; I don't get home till two. He loves the outdoors; I get hives from too much fresh air. He has a map showing every health food restaurant in the city; I know the shortcut to Donut Hut.

But we hung out and *hung in* for years. We went through many phases. There was the I-Can't-Keep-My-Hands-Off-You phase and the If-You-Touch-Me-I'll-Kill-You phase; the Go-Out-With-Somebody-Else phase and the Come-Back-I'm-Miserable-Without-You phase; the Let's-Move-in-Together phase and the I'd-Rather-Be-Buried-Alive-Under-An-Avalanche phase. The only phase we didn't go through was the Pick-Out-a-Wedding-Dress-I'll-Get-the-Ring phase. Ultimately, we settled into that comfortable void known as the Go-Nowhere Sanitarium for the Hopelessly Uncommitted.

Take it from someone who's been there. Before it's too late, *move on*, Fair Princess, or your prince won't be able to find you. You'll be bogged down in the mud with a lingering, loitering, green thing.

A frog doesn't necessarily have to be a jerk, a wimp, or a slimebucket. He can be a great guy. But if he's not the great guy you are going to walk down the aisle with—he's a frog. *Throw him back into the pond!*

The Really-Nice-Guy-But-Really-Bad-Kisser Frog

Sorry, ladies, but if you don't like the way he kisses, he's a frog. You can't teach kissing. It either works or it doesn't. He slobbers too much. Or it's so dry he gives you blisters. Keep him as a friend. If you don't like kissing him, don't even *think* about getting into bed with him.

If he drools, spits or makes you wince—this guy is definitely not your prince.

The Married Frog

He says he's getting a divorce. They just live together for convenience. Her mother is ill. The kids will be out of school soon. Ribbet, ribbet, ribbet.

Whether or not he wears a wedding band, if he's married—*you're* going to end up with warts!

Okay, I'm guilty. I've dated a married man. More than once. More than *one*. But I swear I'll never do it again.

When I met Jeff, he didn't tell me he was married. (Did I mention I slept with him the first night? Oops!)

In fact, he never mentioned the "M" word. One of his friends did: "I saw you at Canter's with Jeff the other day. You know he's married, don't you?"

"Oh, sure," I lied, after casually letting out a deafening primal scream. "Jeff and I were just talking shop."

On our third "date," Jeff was shocked when he came over, expecting me to sleep with him again, and I said no. I confronted him: "Why didn't you tell me you have a wife?"

His answer was classic: "I didn't think you'd go out with me if you knew."

Seems reasonable, right? Except by then, I was hooked. I knew he was married and I kept seeing him. Oh, at first I said I wouldn't. Alas, my conviction was strong but my flesh was weak. What can I say? We had desire, lust, passion—we were on fire!

It was tumultuous and painful. When I'd go to the comedy club where we'd met, Jeff would pretend not to know me. (Oh, *that* felt really good.) One night at the bar, less than 24 hours after we'd had a veritable sex marathon, some-

He's-an-Adulterer/You're-a-Slut/How-Will-It-End?
Relationship Frognosis

He stays married and keeps seeing you on the sly—which means:

NOT on weekends—it's family time.

NOT at Christmas—he's skiing with the clan.

NOT on Valentine's Day—he's at dinner with his wife, the one who doesn't understand him.

NOT on Thanksgiving—he's at his in-laws.

NOT on your birthday—his kid is in the school play.

NOT at all your girlfriends' weddings—no way he'll be seen with you in public. (Maybe he could wear a funny nose and glasses? Hey, he won't look any sillier than you do in those dorky bridesmaids' dresses.)

He gets divorced and divorces you, too.
Come on, he only liked sleeping with you because it was forbidden. Once he's free, he wants to be *free* of you, too. So he sleeps with your girlfriend. (I know the pain.)

He gets divorced and keeps seeing you.
But he vows he'll *never* get married again. His wife took his house, his car and his money. Now he can finally see you on weekends. He just can't afford to take you anywhere!

He marries you and cheats on you.
Why not? He did it with *you*, right?

He's not really married at all.
He just told you he was, so he'd be appealing.

He's married in four different states to four different women.
It's polyfrogamy!

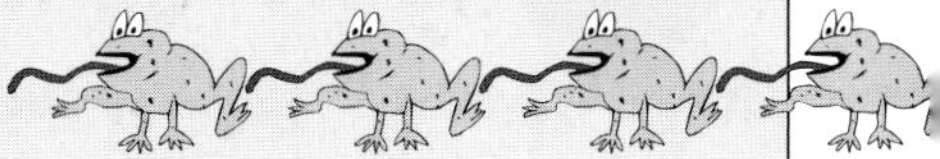

one cheerfully introduced us. Jeff smiled and said, "Oh, where are you from—do you live around here?"

I got so mad, I threw a glass of wine in his face. The only problem was—Jeff stepped aside and it splashed all over the girl standing next to him. Thank God it was *white* wine. (I offered to pay her cleaning bill even though I think Jeff should have paid it.) In retrospect, she was quite lucky. If she hadn't left to go wash up, Jeff might've started dating *her*.

The end of the story? Jeff finally did get divorced. His wife was crushed. But guess what? Within a year, she was remarried.

And what did I get? Well, I got Jeff—for a while. What I didn't get was the "M" word. What I didn't get was a prince.

Toadally True Stories

When you're out in the world, men don't always tell you that they're married. So when you meet a guy, it's crucial to ask. However, even when you ask, sometimes the answers get muddled.

Frog	I Said	He Said	What He *Didn't* Say
Ross:	Are you attached?	Not at the moment.	My wife is away for the weekend.
Steve:	Are you single?	I'm divorced.	From wife # 1—but I'm still married to wife # 2.
Brad:	Are you married?	I'm separated.	For an hour. My wife's getting her hair done—how 'bout a 59-minute quickie?
Kyle:	Are you available?	Yes, I'm yours forever.	Or at least until next week when I get married. My fiancée is at the caterers, so I have the night free. And she's tied up with wedding plans all week, so I squeeze you in a few other nights, too.
Ted:	Are you married?	Yes, but we have an arrangement.	If you can arrange to see me, I can arrange to get out of the house.
Jordan:	Are you married?	Yes, but I have an open marriage.	If you'll open your legs, I'll overlook my marriage.
Brian:	If you're married, why are you at a singles bar?	My wife is in a mental institution.	She works there nights, so I can go out and pick up chicks.
Wes:	If you're married, why are you asking me out?	My wife doesn't like sex.	How would you feel about spanking me with a paddle and an electric prod?
Zak:	How does your wife feel about your dating?	I have her permission to meet other women.	She wants me to bring one home for a ménage à trois.

The Horny Toad

Let's get something straight. I like sex. No, correction: I love sex. (Especially when it's with someone I *like*.) However, I must admit, even when it's with someone I *love*, once in a rare while:

I'm not in the mood. Or . . .
I'm tired. Or . . .
I have a headache. (Honest, sometimes I really *do* get them!)

The Horny Toad doesn't care. He wants sex when *he* wants sex! It doesn't matter what you want. Or when. He won't take no for an answer. He wants to jump you, hump you, pump you and thump you 24 hours a day. He's forever pinching, pulling, poking, squeezing, goosing, tugging, tweaking and nipping at parts of your body. Whether you're alone, or in a crowd. Or across the table from Mom and Dad. Isn't it more exciting that way? Duh—not always.

So what do you say to a Horny Toad? Two words: *"Frog Off!"*

18

Thirteen Horny Toad Tip-Offs

1. He doesn't understand the word "No." Or "Not now." Or "Later." Or, "Goddamn it, leave me alone—my cat just died!"

2. You always look like you just got off a horse.

3. His fingerprints are permanently embedded in your butt.

4. You have to carry a pillow to sit on.

5. When you go to parties, the hosts announce: "The Rabbits have arrived."

6. He humps you on the conference room table—while the conference is in progress.

7. He's got a perpetual *erection*; you—a constant *yeast infection.*

8. You do it in elevators. Now that sounds good, right? But you also do it on escalators, ski lifts and surfboards. At weddings and baptisms. He humps you in the confessional. (Actually, this can save you time. While you're doing it, yell out "Hail Mary!")

9. At department stores, when the sales clerks see you coming, they barricade the dressing rooms.

10. He likes to do it on airplanes, trains, subways, buses, and trolleys—in fact, on all kinds of public transportation—he's a "transit-sexual!"

11. When you come over, your friends put plastic covers on their furniture.

12. You get thrown out of the library, but not for talking.

13. He insists on going with you to pick out (i.e. to *try out*) your uncle's casket!

Frognote: Give this guy some nice parting gifts: a cold shower, a pound of liver, a Pamela Anderson blow-up doll.

Just be prepared, after you've dumped him, there's a good chance your girlfriends will ask for his phone number.

The Indy Froghundred

Dave was a fix-up. Some married friends of mine thought we would hit it off because we had mutual interests. We both loved the theater. And we both liked to eat. Dave would be the perfect person for me to date. Besides, my friends told me, "He has a Porsche!" But instead of that *impressing* me, it ended up *distressing* me.

Dave was a lunatic in his Porsche. He'd zoom through the streets, over the freeway, like Evil Knievel on amphetamines. His driving drove me crazy. I'd continually ask him to slow down. Even when he did, it wouldn't help. He would zip in and out of lanes, squeezing through spaces not wide enough for dental floss. He'd constant-ly make short stops, frantically zigzag, then vehemently careen and jerk around sharp turns, reminding me of my most feared and hated roller coaster: the Cyclone!

To make matters worse, Dave had Road Rage. Or in this case, *Toad* Rage. Every time another car passed him, his fists would clench, his eyes would bulge, and a slew of horrific curse words would spew out his window to the offending driver. It was terrifying. I didn't know which to be more afraid of—Dave showing off behind the wheel, swerving into oncoming traffic and causing a 20-car pile-up—or Dave *getting shot* behind the wheel, swerving into oncoming traffic and causing a 20-car pile-up.

Either way, I was going to end up in a deep, meaningful relationship—with an airbag!

Dave understood my phobia; he just couldn't abide by it. Let's face it, ladies: A man's Porsche isn't just his car. A man's Porsche is

his penis. And he thinks if he can get us *in* it, he can get *it* in us.

In a world of frogs, I'm a chicken. I don't like skydiving, parasailing, bungee jumping, fire walking or speeding. Some girls do. Look for Dave's license plate on the freeway:

TOADSYLVANIA

RRRIBBET

Save the Frogs   2003

The Mama's Frog

I'm always wary of grown men who live with a roommate. But it's especially scary when a grown man introduces you to the *marvelous woman* he lives with: his mother!

"It's great," Bob told me. "She cooks, cleans, takes my phone messages, and we keep each other company."

Well, as far as I was concerned, three's a crowd, and that was the time for *me* to hop away.

If you have any doubts, here are ten clues that you might be dating a Mama's Frog:

1. He gives you his mother's meatloaf recipe. Just to make sure you don't screw it up, he brings her along to cook it.

2. When he takes you both for a ride, he

insists his mother sit in the front. This is a particularly bad sign if his car is a two-seater.

3. His mother knits all his sweaters. They have matching *booties*.

4. He has M-O-M tattooed on his arm—and his leg—and his butt!

5. He invites you to an amusement park and brings mom along. In the Tunnel of Love, he kisses *her*.

6. His favorite movie is *Psycho*.

7. The only part of his house he keeps clean is the shrine to his mother.

8. During sex, he calls out his mother's name.

9. He has her picture in his wallet, on the mantel and over his bed.

10. He brings his mother on all your dates. She's in an urn.

Throw Mama from the pond—and her spawn back into it.

Ribbet Snippet

If he's got excess "Mother Love," find yourself another love!

TOADSYLVANIA
RRRIBBET
Save the Frogs 2003

Did You Hear the One about the Frog Who . . .

Rodney was a blind date. My girlfriend Cheryl had sworn he was adorable. Handsome, successful and funny. She'd emphasized "funny." Now, I *love* funny. I love to laugh. But hopefully it's because we're laughing together. Having fun. Sharing incredibly witty repartee. The only problem: It didn't happen *quite* that way.

I answered the door. Ta-da! Rodney stood there. He was handsome, all right. About six-feet-two, trim and tan. With chiseled good looks. I was already planning to send Cheryl an appropriate "Thank you." This guy was a hunk! I'd do her dishes for the next two weeks. I'd buy her groceries! Maybe I'd even give her that blue silk blouse of mine she constantly lusted after.

I grabbed my coat, and we headed out the door. Rodney was taking me to a new Italian restaurant. The one I had been dying to go to. This was *it*! In my head, I was planning our wedding.

We hadn't even gotten to the car yet when he started his shtick: "Two guys walk into a bar . . ." He actually *said* that. In fact, he said it three times. In three different jokes. Three different *really bad* jokes. (Did you ever hear a good joke that started that way?) And that was just the beginning of the evening. There were more bad jokes,

Ribbet Snippet

If he always tells crude, tasteless jokes don't introduce him to your folks.

TOADSYLVANIA
RRRIBBET
Save the Frogs   2003

old jokes, dirty jokes and ethnic jokes. There were Polish jokes, bald jokes, short jokes and deaf-mute jokes. Even a short, bald, Polish deaf-mute joke. And you know what? Rodney *liked* me. He was doing it to impress me! With how *funny* he was.

Jokes to me are not funny. They are boring. Jokes are something that guys tell each other at conventions. Or in locker rooms. Or in countless, round-the-clock e-mails designed to use up valuable space on your hard drive and surreptitiously infect your computer with some devastating virus!

But on a date, maybe one joke, possibly two, are bearable (barely). But joke after joke? That's *not* funny.

Nor is it a "sense of humor." Did you ever notice how men's personal ads always say they have a "great sense of humor?" The personals even have an abbreviation for it: SOH. The guys have an "SOH" and they always want a woman with an "SOH." Does telling jokes mean he has an SOH? No! It means he has NTS: *nothing to say.*

Also, just because guys like to go to comedy clubs doesn't mean they have a sense of humor. Or that they are funny. Now, don't get me wrong, comedy clubs can be fun—but not when your date is *memorizing the material* to repeat on the way home. And on your phone machine the next day. And the next! Rodney left me six of these repeat-what-the-comic-said messages before I finally told him I had started seeing someone else: a bald, Polish, deaf-mute pygmy I had met at the Christian Science Reading Room.

In summary, beware of the man who woos you with jokes. He's not funny; he's deluded. He thinks *you'll* think he has a sense of humor.

And now, there's just one more thing to say: "Two frogs walk into a bar . . ."

The Thinks-Flattery-Will-Get-Him-Everywhere Frog

A variation of the man who constantly tells jokes is the man who constantly *compliments* you. Now, don't misunderstand, I think I'm funny, sexy, smart, adorable—all those things. And I like it when someone notices. And even tells me—sometimes. But when a man does nothing but flatter me all night, it means one of two things:

1. He has nothing else to say.

2. He can't even memorize a joke.

A conversation is important. If all a man does is tell you how beautiful you are, it can get real dull, real fast. Of course, if you're a narcissist, maybe you like someone who does this. But I prefer an exchange of ideas, common inter-

ests and scintillating dialogue. (A nice bulge in his pants isn't bad, either.) Even if a man is the proverbial strong, silent type or somewhat shy and reserved, he's better company than an indiscriminate, incessant brownnoser.

Example: Perry the Praiser. He arrived at my door to take me bicycling. "You look fantastic," he said. "I love that outfit."

"Thanks." I smiled.

"What gorgeous legs you've got!" Once again I beamed, knowing my early years of tap dancing had paid off. Then Perry complimented me on my apartment, my furniture and my toilet paper.

We headed out, whereupon he raved about the paint job on my bicycle (which was my next door neighbor's) and the color of my helmet (also my neighbor's). Maybe I should have fixed him up with my neighbor, who actually might have liked his compliments. (My neighbor is a

250-lb. sweet, lonely gay guy.)

Whereas Perry was athletic, I am a major klutz. Nonetheless, when I fell and hideously scraped my shins, he told me how *adorable* I looked. "Road rash looks really cute on you. You bleed so bubbly." Later, he told me I bruised in "nice patterns." They were the prettiest black and blue marks he'd ever seen!

At dinner, I ate "cute," I held my fork "enchantingly" and I sipped my drink "in the most delightful way." When he dropped me off, Perry reminded me that he loved my hair, he'd never seen such big brown eyes and my lips were absolutely perfect.

As I closed the door, I felt an overwhelming urge to call my ex (a.k.a. "The Critical Frog") just so I could feel *some* emotion other than pure, unadulterated *boredom*. It worked. My old beau answered the phone and within seconds uttered, "Have you lost some weight?" "Did you get that liposuction?" and "You're a pain in the ass!"

"Thank you," I said. Then I hung up the phone feeling much better.

Ribbeting Experiences

The Obsessed-With-His-Body Frog

We know women can get obsessed with dieting. But women aren't the only ones, believe me.

Alec was in good shape. He ran. He worked out. He was buff. And to top it off, he seemed sincere, charming, and—dare I say it?—debonair. A chivalrous man in an un-chivalrous age. The day after we met, he called and invited me out for a "romantic" dinner. *Whoaaa!* I thought. This guy is about to sweep me off my feet.

I must have changed clothes half a dozen times before our date. One dress was cute but not sexy enough. One was too wild, the next too conservative. I finally decided on an elegant black skirt and velvet jacket that simply oozed "romance."

The doorbell rang. I hurried to greet my knight in shining armor. But there at the front door stood my knight—in shorts and a tank top!

Alec had *underdressed* to impress. He was very proud of his physique and liked to show it off. Especially since he was a former fatty. He'd worked hard to get those pecs and quads, and he wanted the world to see them—*all* of them, all of the time.

As we pulled up to the valet at the as-promised romantic restaurant, Alec pulled a sports jacket from the back seat. And he wore it into the restaurant. But in the booth, ten minutes later, he remarked how "positively warm" it was. (Meanwhile, I was shivering from the icy gusts blasting from the overhead air vent.) He oh-so-casually removed his jacket, once again exhibiting his magnificent, beefy biceps. The romantic portion of the evening had begun.

Alec talked and talked about his fat years: his childhood as a pudgeball, his adolescence as the class tubster, his camp days as Chunky Trunks, and his college nights as Lard Ass. Over time, he'd tried every diet there ever was. Finally, at age 37, he had found a way: daily gym, manic exercise and super-strict eating habits. I was about to find out *how* super-strict.

The waitress came. Alec ordered twigs, leaves and bark. Well, practically. He asked for "skinless chicken breast with lettuce on the side, no dressing, and broccoli steamed in water—with no butter or cheese on anything. And when they steam the broccoli," he emphasized, "absolutely *no oil* in the water."

He confided in me. "I can always tell when they add oil to the water. If I see oil, it goes back." He leaned over and romantically whispered in my ear, "And her tip goes down."

After we sipped some wine, the meal arrived. Alec eyed his plate carefully. He moved his head down to table level and scrutinized the broccoli. Yes, that's right, *scrutinized*. He ran his finger over the broccoli to feel if there was even a smidgen of oil. Finally, he raised his head and gave the okay sign. (Thank God, the waitress could live!)

Then, Alec opened his shoulder bag and took out a scale. I kid you not. He put the scale on the table and weighed his food. The chicken. The broccoli. And yes, he weighed the lettuce. "Fat Busters," he explained. "I'm only allowed to have a certain number of ounces of anything."

"Lettuce?" I asked. "I thought it took more calories to chew it than it gave you."

"Fallacy," he said, cautiously measuring with the delicate scale. "Uh-oh, too much!" He removed two and a half leaves, placed them on his napkin and pushed it aside.

As our "romantic" dinner continued, he rambled on about food supplements, endurance formulas and protein powders. He talked about fava beans, garbanzo beans and bean curd. He ended with an oration on the importance of fruits, fruits, fruits and vegetables, vegetables, vegetables! (I didn't know how much more *romance* I could stand.)

Later, as Alec walked me to my door, saying what a great evening it had been, I sadly moved my eyes over his well-toned body up to his handsome face. Suddenly, I blinked uncomfortably. His head had started to morph. Remember Mr. Potato Head? Well, Alec was now Mr. Lettuce Head! His face was a leafy green mass, adorned with broccoli hair, olive eyes, a carrot nose, and a radicchio mouth. His purplish lips parted. "Can I come in?" he asked.

"Not tonight." I politely smiled.

"Well, maybe next time." He winked an olive, and strolled away, flexing his eggplants.

All in all, Alec had described the evening correctly. It had been a veritable *cornucopia* of romance. I simply had no interest in seeing his *zucchini*!

The Bully Frog

He *snapped* at the hostess.
He *yelled* at the waiter.
He *screamed* at the valet.
Wart Warning: You're next!

The Obsessed-With-His-Ex Frog

I can understand how, after I say goodbye to a man , i.e dump him, his next few women really suffer. It's understandable. I'm so irresistible—so hard to forget, so wonderful to remember—that any man will want to talk about me forever. But he should really keep those feelings to himself—especially, though it doesn't seem possible, any unfavorable ones he might have about me.

Likewise, when I'm going out with someone for the first, second or 34th time, I don't want to hear never-ending details about his former girlfriend, fianceé, wife or some still-hot-and-bothered, fuming, frenzied female stalker.

Now, some conversation on exes is okay.

First-date chitchat invariably covers: "Were you married? Ever live with someone?"

Okay, I've even been guilty of: "Why did you break up? What happened? What was your longest relationship?"

I'm not talking about generic dialogue. I'm talking about the man who constantly obsesses about his ex. He tells you where they used to go, what they did, what she wore, how she still calls him, how she still *loves* him! He may take you to a restaurant and say they used to go there. She loved it or she hated it. He shows you her picture. He plays her favorite songs. When she has called, he makes you listen to her message on the answering machine. Then he starts to weep.

It may be that it's too soon for him to be dating after the breakup. Maybe he's truly in pain. Fine. Recommend a therapist. But if he's someone you're dating, you don't want to hear it.

One of the worst Obsessed-With-His-Ex experiences I know of happened to a girlfriend of mine. Becky was dating a new guy. She didn't heed my warning that I thought Paul talked about his last girlfriend a little too much.

Becky liked this man, and didn't want to give him up. Actually, she liked his body; she's very into the physical thing. So, one night—it's finally *the* night—they're in bed, kissing, writhing, getting hot. Suddenly, Paul reaches over to the stereo and flips on a cassette. Emanating full blast from the loudspeakers are the gasping and panting sounds of hot and heavy sex. "Wow, isn't that hot?" he growls as he gropes Becky's butt.

Becky was surprised at hearing the tape. She was even more surprised to learn that it was Paul and his previous girlfriend. He had secretly taped sex with his ex.

Paul later told Becky that, just to get back at his ex, he had sent a copy of the tape to her new boyfriend. "Let's see him try to top *that*!" Paul bragged.

Luckily, Becky escaped from his bed before he had a chance to tape *her*.

Another one of my girlfriends, Kim, was going out with a guy whose previous girlfriend was stalking him. Greg called Kim for a favor one night. He had gotten a restraining order on his ex, and he wanted Kim to deliver it. (Oh, so instead of Greg getting shot, Kim would.)

Okay, these are both extreme examples. But you get the picture.

Thwart-a-Wart: If he can't get *her* out of his mind, get *him* out of yours.

Sir Frogalot

ONCE UPON A TIME on a summer's eve, Lady Guinevere was riding through the forest in the kingdom known as Camelot. Alas, danger befell her! A band of thieves attacked her carriage and ransacked it. She was left stranded by the road. Suddenly, a brave and dashing man appeared out of the mist on his white horse. 'Twas Lancelot. He rescued the fair Guinevere and returned her safely to her kingdom, whereupon he professed his undying love to her.

Ah, Sir Lancelot! What a romantic hero! I vowed I'd find my own someday. And why not? They say history repeats itself. And it did—sort of.

ONCE UPON A TIME on a summer's eve, Lady Marilyn was riding through the streets in the jungle known as Los Angeles. Alas, danger befell her! A bunch of nails attacked her tire and flattened it. She was left stranded by the road. Suddenly, a brave and dashing man appeared out of the mist in his white SUV. 'Twas Harry. He rescued the fair Marilyn and changed her tire, whereupon he professed (no, not undying love) a desire to take her to dinner. She accepted.

Ah yes, it was a magnificent beginning. Harry was to be *my* Sir Lancelot.

The first night, after dinner we went back to his house and listened to opera. It was so romantic. And on our second date, he read me poetry, deep meaningful verse by Yeats. It was even more romantic.

Harry was fun, handsome and smart. He liked opera. He liked poetry. And he liked me.

So I slept with him.

CUT TO THE BEDROOM:

He had great equipment (a large protruding sword).

Perfect, you think.

You think wrong. (His sword went flat, faster than my tire did!)

But I gave him the benefit of the doubt. After all, first times can be awkward. Except, here's where history *did* repeat itself.

Does the term "Wham Bam Thank you Ma'am" sound familiar? Actually, I admit there was a little foreplay, but it was all me "foreplaying" with him.

However, he was a genuinely nice guy, so I decided to discuss it with him.

We kept seeing each other.

CUT BACK TO THE BEDROOM:

Like Avis, he tried harder. The "Wham Bams" lasted a little longer; it was his other bedroom behavior I ultimately couldn't live with. (I'm sure Lady Guinevere wouldn't have, either.)

At the very height of passion, that climactic moment of ecstasy, Harry would always yell out some "special" words. Now, I can understand when couples hop in the sack for the first time, a man might hold back with professions of deep feelings and intimacy. But even after six months of sleeping with me, Harry's most profound exclamations of orgasmic rapture were:

1. "Yikes!"
2. "Holy Moly!"
3. "Hello, Dolly!"

I'm not saying a man has to cry out "I love you!" or "Oh, love of my life!" or "You are my one and only forever." But Yikes, Holy Moly and Hello, Dolly? It sounded like dialogue from a porno cartoon!

So much for my delusions of romance and of undying love. And Sir Lancelot!

On Harry's behalf, I must say that during one lovemaking session, he did manage to say the magic word, "love." But don't get excited. It wasn't "I love you." No. He said, "I love *it*." Call me crazy, but I don't like being an "it" or providing an "*it*."

I finally left Harry. The truth is, I'm not really that fussy. I would've settled for him calling out my name or even the noncommittal "Oh yes!" or "Oh God!" or maybe even "Bingo!" But I just couldn't bear any more of his unique "erotic" sweet talk. So the last time we were together in the throes of passion, when he yelled out, "Hello, Dolly," I simply yelled back, "Goodbye, Kermit!"

Ribbet Snippet

Milady, if at night your knight yells out: Yikes, Zap, or Pow

He's surely a royal frog who is in no way worthy of thou!

The Uncouth Frog

I met Elliot at a comedy club, The Improvisation. He was a comic, a writer and an actor—all signs of imminent danger. Nonetheless, I couldn't resist. He was funny, handsome and sexy—unlike most comics, who are bitter, lonely and angry.

I'd see Elliot hanging out at the bar before and after his act. We'd always make eye contact, smile and flirt. Finally, he asked me out. I had goose bumps galore.

Date night arrived. We did the proverbial dinner and a movie at the mall. We talked; we laughed; we even held hands. I was aflame. Then we went down to the parking garage to get his car.

Suddenly, Elliot had to go to the bathroom. And it seems he couldn't wait. Behind a concrete pole in the parking garage, he "took a leak." Believe me, I've always *hated* that expression, but it wasn't mine, it was his—as in "Jesus, I gotta take a leak!"

Call it what you will—see a man about a horse, make a pit stop, take a whiz, drain a vein, make a siss, pee, piss, whatever—I'm happier when I don't have to see it or smell it on the first date. Or subsequent dates.

I let him know I didn't care for his "out-of-bladder" experience.

"Hey," he said, "In Europe, men do it on the street all the time! Why do you think they have canals in Venice?"

"Oh, that's why!" I responded sarcastically. Somehow I couldn't imagine Prince William doing *that*. And I certainly know *my* prince wouldn't do it!

Anyway, if you're out with a man and he takes a leak in the garage, in the bushes or on the street, he's uncouth. Also, if he swears, slobbers or spits.

And there are other *slime signs*. Hearing about how a man loves his pets is always reassuring—except when over dinner he gives you graphic details about his Great Dane's "deposits." Somehow, Beef Stroganoff doesn't taste quite as good when you're hearing how that afternoon his dog, Duke, required a super duper pooper-scooper.

Beware if a man draws attention to any liquid or solid expelled by the body—his or his pet's. Or anything that drips, sprays or spews. Also crude is scratching of the balls. If a man constantly rubs his crotch, at the end of the night, instead of a kiss, give him a bottle of Cruex.

Another sign of uncouth is if when he is with you, he's constantly ogling other women: checking out their jugs, butts or other parts of their bods as they walk by. Worse, is mentioning it to you: "Wow, did you catch the boobs on that babe?"

"No, I didn't notice." Except I really did—and I was sure they were Silicone City.

So ladies, here's the latest update for **The Wart Report:** The first time a man swears, ogles, gawks or takes a wayward leak, make it your last date. The man is a frog!

The Frog with the Frog in his Throat

He's non-communicative.
He doesn't share his inner feelings
Or his inner thoughts.
Until he gets in touch with his *inner tadpole*
You'll be the one all choked up!

Vive Le Frog!

André— was French. And fabulous. He showered me with romance. Flowers. And love notes! Then, on our one-month anniversary, he proposed: "I can't wait. I want you. I need you. Let's get married right away!"

I was ecstatic until I found out that he didn't need me; he needed a *Green Card*.

He was a "Frog" Frog!

The night I dumped him, instead of ice cream, I ate frogs' legs flambé.

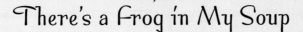

There's a Frog in My Soup

INGREDIENTS:

Raw nerves
Sour moods
Bitter feelings

Crushed hopes
Dried tears
Bottled-up emotions
Burnt bridges

Greasy moves
Coarse habits
Tough talk
Rough edges

Roving eyes
Loose lips
Frog heart
Frog's legs

PREPARATION:

Take the bundle of *raw nerves* (that you've become) and throw it in a pot. Add all his *sour moods* and *bitter feelings*. Dice up all your *burnt bridges*, and add them to the mix.

In a separate bowl, toss your *crushed hopes*, *dried tears* and *bottled-up emotions*—and put them aside.

Break off his *tough talk*, add his *greasy moves*, and whip his *rough edges* till they're mush. Blend them into the pot, along with his *roving eyes*. With a rolling pin, flatten his *loose lips*, and slip them into the mixture. Beat vigorously.

Chop up all his *coarse habits*. Put them into a Mixmaster and mash into a pulp. Add mash to pot. Stir until it simmers.

Put the *Frog's legs* on the side of the hot pot, and let the steam rise so he can feel the heat. Add the *Frog's heart*—if he ever *had* one—and let it all come to the boiling point.

Now, stop stewing. And throw this garbage down the drain! This is one dish where you don't want any leftovers.

Frognote: Don't kiss the frog or you'll end up in the soup.

The Full-of-Bull Frog

He says he's worth millions and pretends that he's a hero.

But he has no pot to pee in, and he really is a zero.

He brags he's friends with Tiger Woods and he has dated Britney Spears.

The truth is he's perpetually blowin' smoke out of his ears.

His Rolex is a fake and he borrowed the Mercedes.

And his estate in Beverly Hills? He rents a room from two old ladies!

He boasts of skiing the Alps and sunning in the south of France,

When he's really gone nowhere (it's all a song and dance).

Everything he says is macho lies and fabrication.

This man is not a *prince*; he's a king of verbal masturbation!

section three

Frog Family Album

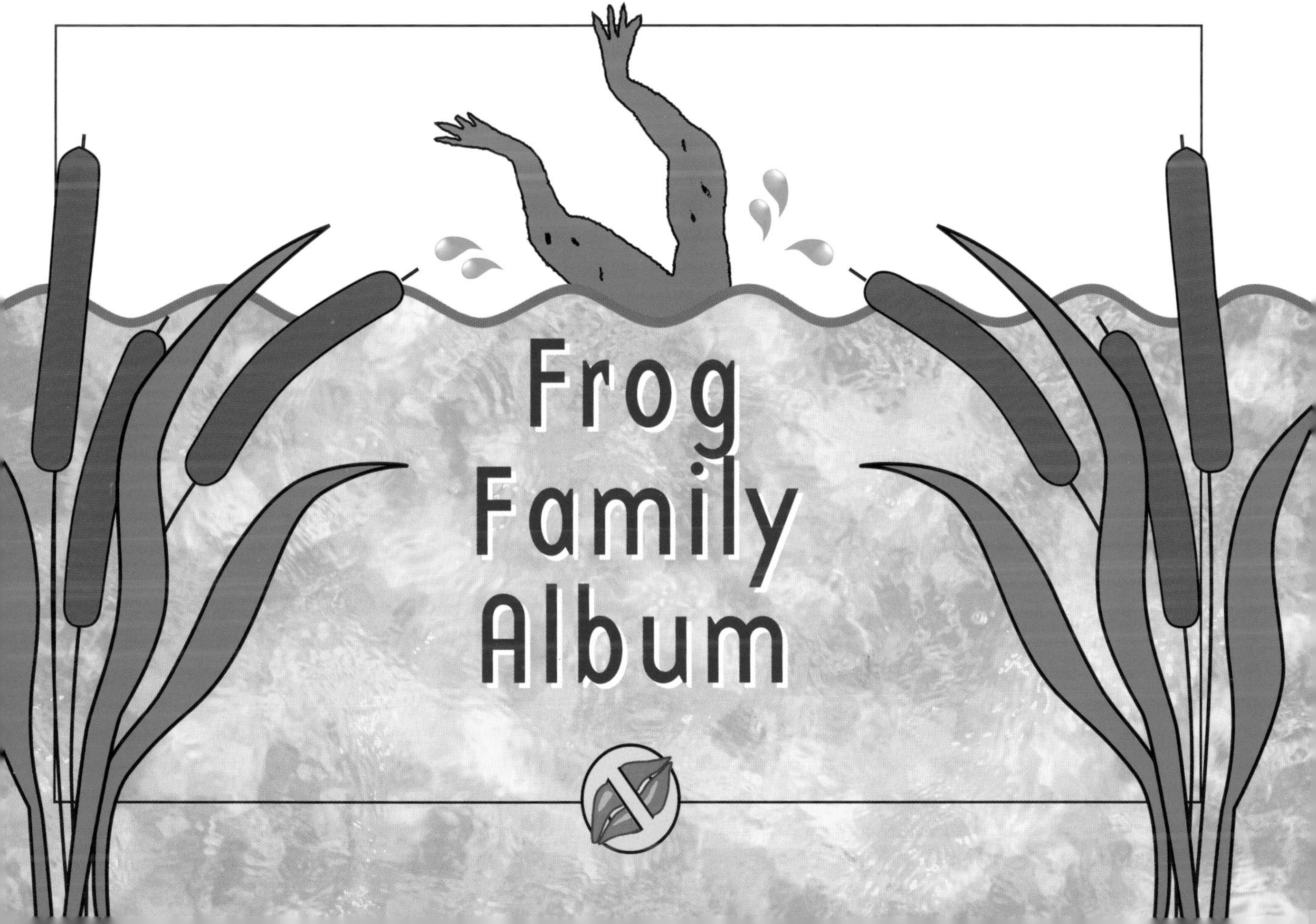

Gone with the Warts Gallery

The Long-Term-Go-Nowhere Frog

The Married Frog

The Horny Toad

Ribbeting Experiences Gallery

The-Obsessed-With-His-Ex Frog

Vive La Frog

The-Obsessed-With-His-Body Frog

43

Frogzilla!

ATTACK OF THE GREEN-EYED MONSTER

SEE his jealous rampage!

HEAR him accuse you of flirting when you're not!

WATCH as he crushes any man you talk to!

SCREAM as he makes you surrender all your friends!

CRY as he holds you captive on his giant lily pad!

Next week's collector's issue: Breaking Free of His Clutches, Call on FROGBUSTERS!

Scrooge McFrog

$ $ $

People marry for it. Divorce over it. Hide it. Hoard it. Lose it. Win it. Steal it. *Kill* for it.

Face it—relationships are often made or broken over cold hard cash.

From the start, you can see how a man uses, handles, feels about, spends or doesn't spend his moolah. And it's not always the size of his wallet that determines his attitude. A prince might be short on cash, but big on heart!

But the worst thing by far is a mega-millionaire who's a mega-miser! Want to know what it's like to go out with this Scrooge. . .

Play "Frogopoly"

But beware: When you roll the dice, even if you win, you lose.

HOW TO PLAY

Roll the dice and move around the board. When you land on a "Date" or a "Kiss," take a card and see what's in store for you.

DATE-ME CARDS

He takes you to an expensive restaurant. After looking at the prices, he says, "Okay, we'll get one crab cake with two forks."

He invites you away for the weekend. You have to listen to a four-hour timeshare presentation. Afterwards, they give you a free toaster. He keeps it!

He picks you up in his new Jaguar. But he won't pay for Valet Parking. So you have to walk 12 blocks to the restaurant—in the rain. With no umbrella. In your new Manolo Blahniks.

He gives you a gold bracelet for your birthday. It's engraved. But they're not your initials. "No one has to know," he whispers. " I got it back from my ex-girlfriend."

He takes you on a shopping spree. He buys a Gucci sweater, a Versace jacket and Prada slacks—for himself. He buys you a pair of gym socks.

He spends $200 on dinner. He tips the waitress $2.

He takes you on a cruise. Your cabin is in steerage. The ship sinks.

A bouquet of flowers from him arrives at your office. You're overjoyed until you read the card. It says, "Happy Bar Mitzvah, Leo!"

He takes you Christmas shopping and tells you to pick out anything you want—from the clearance rack at the *99 Cents* store.

He whisks you away for a sumptuous, romantic weekend—at Motel Six.

He claims he hates credit cards. He'd rather use cash—except he forgets to bring any. So you end up paying for the expensive meal—for the 10th time.

He invites your parents out for their anniversary and picks them up in his limo. Then he pulls into a McDonald's drive-through and says, "Order anything you want. I've got coupons."

You take him to a friend's dinner party. He brings them a bottle of wine: Thunderbird.

He gives you his old car. The paint is rusted, the upholstery is shredded, and you get a bill for $500 of unpaid parking tickets!

He invites you over to see his prized art collection: Picassos, Renoirs and a framed copy of the *pre-nup*—that all his dates must sign.

He tells you he inherited his money from his ex-wife. She's dead. You find out he *killed* her!

KISS-ME CARDS

Close your eyes and pucker up. Then flip the card and watch as your frog turns into a—whoops! Sorry, girls—he turns into a pig, a cockroach, a weasel, a scorpion or even a royal jackass. But never *ever* into a prince!

END PLAY

This game comes with stacks of money—but *you* never get to use any!

Wart Warning

A man who's tight with money will be tight with his affection. And, in the bedroom, expect small inflation followed by immediate recession.

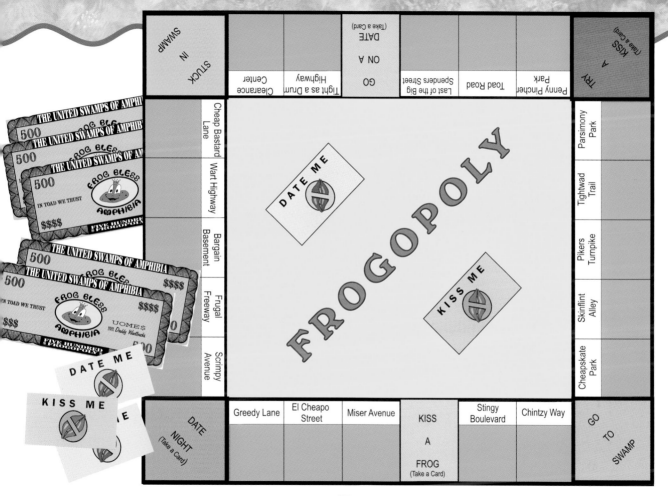

FROGOPOLY

STUCK IN SWAMP

Clearance Center

Tight as a Drum Highway

GO ON A DATE (Take a Card)

Last of the Big Spenders Street

Toad Road

Penny Pincher Park

TRY A KISS (Take a Card)

Cheap Bastard Lane

Wart Highway

Bargain Basement

Frugal Freeway

Scrimpy Avenue

DATE ME

KISS ME

Parsimony Park

Tightwad Trail

Pikers Turnpike

Skinflint Alley

Cheapskate Park

DATE NIGHT (Take a Card)

Greedy Lane

El Cheapo Street

Miser Avenue

KISS A FROG (Take a Card)

Stingy Boulevard

Chintzy Way

GO TO SWAMP

THE UNITED SWAMPS OF AMPHIBIA
500
FROG BLESS
IN TOAD WE TRUST
AMPHIBIA
$$$$
FIVE HUNDRED

47

NEVER KISS A FROG

Count Frogula

Any guy who drains the life out of you—sucks.

The Frog Who's a Rat

Kent and I had been going steady for a year when one of my girlfriends asked me if he had a twin. "No, why do you ask that?" I queried. My girlfriend reluctantly told me: "I saw his photo on Match.com. Only there, he calls himself *Frank*!"

I call him Frog.

This rat without *loyalty* definitely isn't *royalty*!

If you keep dating *rats*, you'll get stuck in the maze—and never find your prince.

Help! Where's my prince?

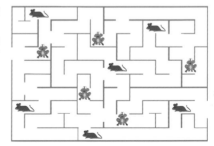

Guess I'll have to ride off into the sunset without her

48

The Frog Who's a Snake

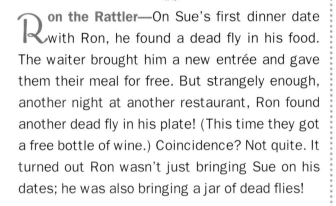

Ron the Rattler—On Sue's first dinner date with Ron, he found a dead fly in his food. The waiter brought him a new entrée and gave them their meal for free. But strangely enough, another night at another restaurant, Ron found another dead fly in his plate! (This time they got a free bottle of wine.) Coincidence? Not quite. It turned out Ron wasn't just bringing Sue on his dates; he was also bringing a jar of dead flies!

Pete the Python—Pete was enchanting, devilishly handsome, and the perfect man to show off to Kelly's friends. So she held parties where everyone could meet him. Months later, her girlfriends discovered that their credit cards had excessive charges. It seems that, during the parties, Pete would slither into their purses, write down their credit card numbers, and use them for mail-order shopping. Pete was a guy who gave snakes a bad name!

Vic the Viper—Liz wasn't quite ready to have sex with Vic. But she gave in after he confessed to her that he only had three months to live. A couple of weeks later, he broke up with her, saying that he didn't want her to see him suffer with his brain tumor. Amazingly, two years later, Liz saw Vic at a party. He was using his "three months to live" line on another girl. The miracle is that Liz didn't kill him right then and there!

Dave the Diamondback—When Meg moved to a new house, Dave helped her unpack boxes and organize her drawers. He also helped her file the police report the next week when all her jewelry disappeared. Strangely enough, Meg's jewels weren't the only things that disappeared. Meg never again heard from *Dave the Diamondback*—

NEVER KISS A FROG

and she never ever got her diamonds back!

Mike the Moccasin—Tara was redecorating her apartment. Mike told her that his friend with a furniture store would give her a good deal. It was a good deal, all right—for Mike. On everything *she* bought, *he* got a kickback. Too bad she didn't buy a Snake Bite Kit!

Cory the Cobra—Cindy told Cory she'd only sleep with him if they had a monogamous relationship. He swore she was his "one and only." And he told her he'd had a vasectomy. After they'd been lovers for four months, she got a call from his *other* "one and only." Not only wasn't he monogamous, he was polyfrogamous! Worse, both Cindy and the other "one and only" were pregnant. Cory had lied about his vasectomy, too. This two-timing snake was so fertile he could have opened his own Sperm Bank!

Bob the Boa—Bob was wearing a neck brace when Eve met him. He said he had whiplash from a car accident. Still, it didn't prevent him from taking her skateboarding. Two months later, Bob showed up in an arm cast from *another* car accident. Either he was very unlucky or a very bad driver. Actually, he was very good—at collecting insurance! Eve finally realized this at Bloomingdale's. She saw Bob deliberately "slip and fall." Before he even hit the ground, he yelled, "Call my lawyer!"

Make sure you don't slip—and fall for a snake like him!

The Frog-Who's-a-Wolf Test

Congratulations! You snagged a big one— the guy who everyone said was a ladies man. But now he has settled down and moved in with you. All the girls are so jealous! He's got a gorgeous bod, a chiseled face and bedroom eyes. But can you be sure they'll stay in *your* bedroom? Take this test and see.

You work late one night. Your boyfriend:

1. Stays home and watches TV
2. Goes out with the guys
3. Calls a phone sex hotline
4. Takes your best friend to dinner— at your favorite restaurant

You introduce him to one of your girlfriends at a party. He:

1. Shakes her hand and says, "Hi. It's nice to meet you."
2. Squeezes you and announces to your pal, "She's the best thing that's ever happened to me."
3. Hugs your friend so tight, she feels the bulge in his pants
4. Says to her, "Want to come home and take a hot tub with us?"

You go on a cruise together and you get seasick. He:

1. Stays in the room and takes care of you
2. Goes ashore and brings you back a present
3. Has an affair with the Social Director
4. Holds a party in the cabin and, when you puke your guts out, says, "Don't mind her."

A girlfriend calls your house when you're away on a business trip. Your boyfriend:

1. Says you're away, but he'll tell her you called
2. Tells her about the surprise party he's throwing for your birthday
3. Starts breathing heavy and asks her, "What are you wearing?"
4. Invites her to go to an S & M club

Your gorgeous mom has you over for dinner. While you're in the bathroom, he:

1. Thanks her and helps her wash the dishes
2. Asks her if she knows what ring size you wear
3. Gives her a big "thank you" kiss— all over her body
4. Gives her the Heimlich Maneuver even though she's not choking

At the beach, a voluptuous girl in a string bikini loses her top. Your boyfriend:

1. Acts as if he doesn't notice
2. Tells you, "You're much prettier than her."
3. Snaps his Speedo and says, "I better go help her."
4. Whips out his camera and takes pictures of her boobs

SCORING

On each of these: If you chose **1.** or **2.**, he might be a prince for you, but if it was **3.** or **4.**, you've got a wolf at your door! He *scores* and you lose points.

The Frog Who's a Wolf in Sheep's Clothing

By day he seemed quite nice and kind and even awfully shy.

But nights brought out his mean, cruel streak—a scary kind of guy.

At work he wore conservative suits, was polite and quite tight-laced.

But on dates he was tattooed, with rings and piercings strategically placed!

His body art had skulls and knives and weapons of fear and loathing.

This wasn't my sweet prince at all but a frog who's a wolf in sheep's clothing!

The Frog Who's a Frog in Prince's Clothing

If he *looks* like a prince and *dresses* like a prince, he just might be a frog *in disguise.*

The night you met was heavenly. Your first date was *Paradise.* Your "first time" was Nirvana. This man is your prince!

Don't be so sure.

Remember, at the beginning, even *frogs* are on their best behavior. It's usually not until three months into the relationship that their webbed feet begin to show. Okay, so you realize that your prince has a few flaws. Hey, no one's perfect. So he won't go to your parents' house for dinner. You can accept that. (You don't want to go, either.) So he brings his dog on your dates. You can live with that. (Unfortunately, he brings his dog into bed, too. You *can't* live with that!) And lately, there are lots of things you'd like to live *without*. Those little things are getting bigger and bigger. And they're starting to make you squirm.

Relax. Take a deep breath. Come on, don't give up the chance to walk down the aisle with your prince! Look at that crown on his head and think about that ring on your finger. Does he deserve a gentle reprimand or the royal guillotine? Should you forgive him or forget him?

As Sir Isaac Newton said, "For every action there is an equal and opposite reaction."

You're sick with a rotten cold. He doesn't bring you chicken soup. Let it pass.

You get a tonsillectomy. He doesn't come to the hospital. *Remove his scepter.*

You go to a big party. He ignores you. Forget it.

You overhear him telling a joke. It's about you! *Remove his royal slippers.*

He stops taking his Prozac. Let it go.

He uses up *your* Prozac. *Remove his royal cape.*

On your birthday, he takes you to a restaurant you hate. Forgive him.

On your anniversary, he takes you to a gay bar. *Remove his crown.*

He secretly snaps pictures of you naked. Laugh about it.

He posts them on the Internet. *Color him green!*

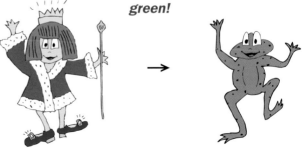

You've heard the story of the frog
that turned into a Prince?
Now you can see, it's the other way around!

Slime Street Gallery

Smokin' and Croakin'

The Godfrogger

Croak and Dagger

Close Encounters Gallery

The Groggy Froggy

All-Play-No-Work Frog

Frog-in-the-Box

Nightmare on Slime Street

Dr. Jekyll and Mr. Frog

What could be better than marrying a prince? Marrying a *doctor*! And I was on my way. I had met a *prince* of a doctor.

Todd was a gynecologist, an eminent Beverly Hills gynecologist with a thriving practice. Women from all over the city lined up in droves to see him.

It was understandable. Todd was gentle, compassionate and incredibly good-looking. Women would take one look at his piercing blue eyes and want to lie back and spread their legs! He was a phenomenon. How often do you hear about patients *looking forward* to climbing into those stirrups?

But I was the lucky one. *They* got his bedside manner. I got him at my *bedside*.

Let me tell you, there are benefits to dating a "gyno." They have trade secrets. Todd was the Captain Kirk of the sexual universe. His mission: "To boldly go where no man has gone before." I'd yell, "More power, Scottie!" And then he'd beam me up. You know how Mr. Spock did the Vulcan Mind Meld? Well, Todd did the *Vulva* Mind Meld!

Of course, I treated him well, too. Knowing he looked at female anatomy all day, I would want mine to look special. So I drew "tattoos" on my tummy. Or wrote messages in lipstick: "Slow, dark tunnel ahead!" and "Go ahead, make my day!"

It was an exciting beginning. I kept thinking about how happy my mother would be introducing him: "My son-in-law, the doctor!"

Alas, everyone knows the saying: "All good things must come to an end." Or that other one: "Shit happens."

It did. As time passed, Todd's charming

bedside manner was often left at the office. He had a bit of a temper. Without warning, the littlest thing could set him off. One minute he'd be sweet and loving, the next he was Hannibal Lecter! I felt as if he would eat me alive. I decided to talk to him about it. With the utmost tact, I said, "You're a schizoid loony psycho. Have you thought about getting help?"

"I did," he responded. "I went to group therapy. I was the only one there, but I have a *multiple personality.*"

I would have laughed, except it was true. I was dating the male Sybil.

Unfortunately, I didn't figure this out until *after* we moved in together. Hey, since he had a split personality, maybe he'd pay two thirds of the rent! Actually, Todd paid it all. But I paid in other ways.

Like at dinnertime. Todd and I could be having a perfectly nice conversation then sud-denly one word would send him ballistic. And he didn't just throw a tantrum; he threw *food.* One night an entire plate of lasagna hit the wall!

Todd quickly calmed down and apologized. He gave his winning, little-boy smile. "Come on, honey, that's not me; it's my evil twin. And look, he's an artist!"

I stared at the lasagna-splattered wall, which now resembled a bad Jackson Pollack painting. We cleaned up in the kitchen, and made up in the bedroom.

If it had just happened once, I could have let it go. But I was beginning to see *less* of Todd and *more* of his evil twin. His bad moods made my PMS seem like Happy Hour.

To relax, he took up a hobby: rearranging furniture—by throwing it. He hurled a lamp, chairs and once the dining room table. That was it! I realized if I stayed with this doctor, I'd *need* a doctor. I flexed my pitching arm. If he could

Frog on the Rocks

If he's a boozer, you're the loser!

60

throw furniture and throw food, I could throw *him* out.

Question: How do you break up with a man who throws things?

Answer: By phone or fax.

And what do you say? "I met someone new." No. "I'm going back with my old boyfriend." *Unh-unh.* "I'm commitment-phobic." (Actually, I'm evil-twin phobic.)

Finally, I just wrote him a letter.

Dear Todd,

Seeing you has been wonderful. But I've realized I'm a lesbian!

Hey, why not? It made sense. If he asked why I had moved in with him, I had the answer: Hearing him talk about his patients turned me on!

So much for Dr. Todd and his evil twin— a.k.a. Dr. Jekyll and Mr. Frog.

Thwart-a-Wart: If a man has a split personality, you should be the one to *split*.

Amphibious and Oblivious Test

1. You've always worn your hair long. But your boyfriend says he likes short hair. So one day, you take the big step. You head to the most expensive beauty salon in town, and get it cut, short and trendy. Your boyfriend:

a. Doesn't notice

b. Says, "I liked it better long."

c. Says, "Why don't you wear a hat?"

d. Says, "Cool, you got a nose job!"

2. You starve yourself for a month. You're all excited. You're down a whole dress size and the scale says you've lost 10 pounds. Your boyfriend:

a. Doesn't notice

b. Says, "You don't look any different."

c. Says, "Let's see if you can keep it off!"

d. Takes you out for a celebration dinner to a soul food restaurant. You have a choice of fried chicken, barbecued ribs, or pork chops with biscuits and gravy!

3. You're going in for one of those not-so-delightful "female" procedures. The doctor says you won't be able to have sex for two months. The night before the procedure, your boyfriend:

a. Watches a ball game

b. Goes out with his buddies

c. Picks a fight with you

d. All of the above

4. For your anniversary, your boyfriend tells you he's taking you somewhere special. The day arrives. You dress in a sexy spaghetti-strap dress and heels. He takes you:

a. To a swap meet

b. Bowling

c. To a nudist colony

d. To be a contestant in a female Mud Wrestling Contest

5. Your boyfriend goes out of town for a week. He can't take you with him because it's a heavy-duty business trip—a trade show for the gift industry. He:

a. Doesn't call

b. Doesn't bring you a gift

c. Doesn't let you know his plane is two hours late, so you are left waiting at the airport

a and **c** : You break down and call his hotel. They never heard of him. There's no trade show in town. His company doesn't exist!

Scoring

The more oblivious he is, the more *warts* you get.

a. = 1 wart

b. = 2 warts

c. = 3 warts

d. = 10 warts.

If you scored 1-5 warts, we'll forgive you. Hey, a good man is hard to find. So apply some wart-away cream and see if you can live with it. If you scored from 6-10 warts, it's not great, but hell, what is? Grit your teeth and use vast amounts of industrial strength *Compound W*. If you scored anywhere between 11-50 points, *you* are oblivious. This man is a definitive big, green, ugly, slimy toad. Take 18 showers and change your phone number. Put phone block on *his* number. And, for God's sake, stay away from his swamp!

E=mc^{frogged}

Multiply the number of times he didn't put the seat down

By the number of times he said he hated your best friend.

Add the number of times he said you'd never make it through grad school.

Divide by the number of times he bought you flowers.

Add the larger of how many times he criticized your driving

Or the number of times he made faces at your cooking.

Take the total—and drive at that speed

Ten times farther away than the number of nights you spent with him.

Croak and Dagger

Your croaker clues:

He won't tell you where he lives;

Where he works;

What he does. He can call *you* but you can't call *him*.

He finally gives you a phone number but it's voice mail

And you have to leave a message.

Maybe he'll call you back,

But don't hold your breath.

Wart Warning

Mystery men can be exciting but if he's mysterious for too long, *you* should be the one to disappear.

The Godfrogger

It was a hot steamy night. I had this noisy air conditioner that was blowin' heat. And my landlord wouldn't fix it. But I had to get some Z s.

It was a losing battle. I was tossing and turning like flapjacks in an earthquake. So I figured, what the heck? I got up and put on this cute little black number. Then I headed over to Guido's, a cool Italian place with a hot piano bar.

I sauntered up to the bar to get a martini. Then I spotted him: the guy at the microphone. He was singing "Strangers in the Night." He sounded like Sinatra and looked like Antonio Banderas. (The *Italian* Antonio Banderas.) And he was staring straight at me. Burning his big brown peepers into my soul. Boom! I'm smitten.

"Tony" is for me!

So I'm trying to be cool, chewing on my olive. But I stab my lip with the toothpick. I scream and drop my purse, spilling the contents. I bend down to scoop up my stuff. But by the time I cram everything back inside the purse, and climb back on my perch, the song is over. Tony is gone. My heart falls.

Suddenly, there's a tap on my shoulder. I turn around. Tony is standing right there at my side—with a cocktail napkin. He blots a drop of blood from my lip.

"Should I kiss it and make it better?" He smiles.

"Maybe later," I answer.

Then I compliment him: "I like your pipes."

"I like your gams."

"I like your suit."

"I like your hair."

"I like your. . ."

He interrupts. "So whattaya say we have dinner?"

"I thought you'd never ask."

We get a table. I order chicken cacciatore. He orders *broken* leg of lamb. That should've been my first clue. But I'm too gaga to notice.

He takes my hand. It's not raining, but I hear thunder and see lightning. As it flashes, I imagine a big Italian wedding. The band is playing our song. Hundreds of guests surround us. They fill my wedding purse with checks and cash. Suddenly, I hear a clink and I'm back to Guido's.

Tony is toasting me with a glass of Chianti:

Wart Warning

If he's a wiseguy, be a wise girl—
Frogeddaboudit!

"To us!"

He tells me, "Singing's just a hobby. I'm a businessman—in construction. Cement."

That should've been my second clue. But right now, the only thing I'm trying to solve is the problem with my heart. It's beating a hundred times a minute. (My brain cells aren't functioning at all.)

We make small talk over dinner. I tell him about the difficulty I'm having with my landlord.

He squeezes my hand comfortingly. "If you want, I'll pay him a visit and break his kneecaps."

I laugh, thinking it's a joke. Then, seeing the seriousness in his deep, dark eyes, I ask, "You wouldn't really do that?"

"Nah, of course not," he says. "Not me—I'll have one of my boys do it." He points to a bruiser at the bar. "Bruno's broken more noses than Mohammed Ali. Ba-da-bing, ba-da-boom!"

Holy olive oil, I think to myself, he's serious. This is an offer I *can* refuse. I shake my head, "That's okay. I'm moving next week, anyway."

I finish my dinner at triple speed. Then I tell him it's been a blast meeting him. But I'm going out of town. On a cruise. With my great aunt. Around the world. For three years.

I give him a peck on the cheek, and leave. You see, even though I love movies about the *mob*, I don't want to be *married* to it.

That night I have a dream. Tony and I are making out. You think it's hard for guys to remove a bra? You should try removing a bulletproof vest!

I never saw Tony again. But I saw his picture in the newspaper. It turned out *he* was the one going away: for five to ten—at Sing-Sing.

A Toadal Makeover

I met Barry at a party. We immediately hit it off. He was fun, handsome, and charming. But was he *Prince Charming?* I was soon to find out.

Now, most people don't think I'm fat. Luckily, I'm not even referred to as zaftig. In fact, some of my friends even think of me as thin. Okay, I hide it well, I know how to dress, and have great legs—it comes from having been a dancer.

But I wasn't thin enough or didn't hide it well enough for Barry. He waited until the second date to let me know his thoughts. We were at a Salsa Club. As we were chatting at the table, I started to nibble on some nacho chips. Barry quickly grabbed my hand and plucked the chip out of it. Then, with a grin, he gazed into my eyes. "You need to diet," he said. "That means no chips! No snacks! " He snatched the bowl, then motioned to the passing waiter. "Take this away."

Take *him* away, I thought.

"You should never eat between meals," he said. "And then, no carbs. And nothing fried." He continued, "You'll look great 10 pounds lighter. Lose 15 and you'll be a knockout!"

I could relate to the knockout part—that's what I wanted to do to him. *Ka-Boom*—right in his tight-toned gut. But I didn't want to cause a scene. Besides, I wanted to dance. Hey, maybe I could sweat off a few pounds.

Now don't get me wrong. I wouldn't mind losing a little weight. What woman would? But I think the "how and when" should be *my* decision, not *his.*

Barry didn't stop at my eating habits. As the evening wore on, he made other suggestions. "You should color your hair. You'd look hot as a blonde."

On the dance floor, he critiqued my clothes: "They should be more tailored. Low-cut tops are out." The music continued. So did he: "You'd look better wearing brighter colors."

Finally, I couldn't take it anymore. I stopped dancing and pulled away. " I don't get it," I said. "If you don't like the way I look, why did you ask me out?"

He smiled and hugged me. "Hey, I'm in real estate. I *like* fixer-uppers!"

I couldn't help laughing. He had to be kidding me!

But back at the table, it became obvious he wasn't. Barry started telling me how much fun it was to find beat-up old houses and renovate them. He had a ball ripping out floors, refinishing walls and refurbishing kitchens. He'd made a bundle, and he loved doing it. He proudly pulled some pictures from his wallet to show me the "before" and "after."

Well, I thought. Sorry to ruin your fun, Barry but this is one project that's about to be foreclosed!

When he dropped me off that night, I considered telling Barry what I thought of him. I didn't. But when he called me a week later, I fibbed and said I was dating someone new. Someone who liked the property "as is!"

Ribbet Snippet

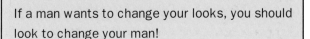

If a man wants to change your looks, you should look to change your man!

Smokin' and Croakin'

John seemed like a great guy. We met. We laughed. We made a date.

He smoked. (A real turn-off for me.) But he said he was quitting. (Maybe he was my prince after all.)

We went out to dinner and then John invited me back to his place to *watch a video*. Keep in mind, ladies: "Watch a video" is frog language. Translation: "I'm going to jump your bones." Now, I'm a normal, healthy woman. I wouldn't want a man who *didn't* want to jump my bones. But usually I'm not ready without at least dinner and a movie first. However, since John had a big-screen TV, I decided that could count as a movie. (Besides which, my bones hadn't been jumped in almost a year!)

And John didn't just have a big-screen TV,

he had a humongous, big-screen TV—in his living room. Except it was more like a dying room. And I was the one dying. His so-called living room was a tiny box, with just enough room for the giant TV, two huge speakers and a long black vinyl couch, only inches from the blinding screen. John told me to get "comfortable" on the couch as he started flipping channels. (You guessed it—he's also a Couch Potato Frog.) And I was supposed to be getting "comfortable." Right! Between being so close to the big screen and the blaring noise, my ears were tingling and my eyes were rolling back in my head. (Usually, this would indicate I was nearing a big "O." In this case, it was a big "Oh no!")

Then, in this teensy-weensy, combination living room/screening room, John lit up! Now the TV was blasting me and a blanket of smoke was enveloping me. About the only way I could've gotten "comfortable" was if I was wearing a blindfold, earplugs and an oxygen mask.

He smiled. "Just one cigarette," he said, as he sexily blew smoke rings in my face. "Then we'll try some romance"

"I'd love some romance," I mumbled, gagging and hacking. "But my inner child has emphysema."

I headed for the door. "Sorry," I gasped between coughs. "But really, I have to get up early, wash my hair, finish a project, write some letters and have a lung removed." I smiled apologetically and left.

John never called again. What can I say? I wish him the best.

But maybe you're a girl who likes it when smoke gets in your eyes. If you're a two-pack-a-day type yourself—and deaf—John might be just the right guy for you. Pick him up at your local Marlboro counter. And here's hoping you have many long months together!

I Toad You So!

If you say black, he says white.
He always has to prove he's right.
No matter what, he has to win—
Whether it's a friendly discussion or a game of gin.

If you say "Roses are red and violets are blue,"
He'll still find a way to make a fool of you.
He'll prove his point and win his case,
Then rub his victory in your face.

Sweet lady, you deserve a prince more gentle,
Not a jerk who's fond of being argumental.
The next time this toad engages you in snippy
  confrontation,
Tell him to pack his attitude and take a perma-
  nent vacation!

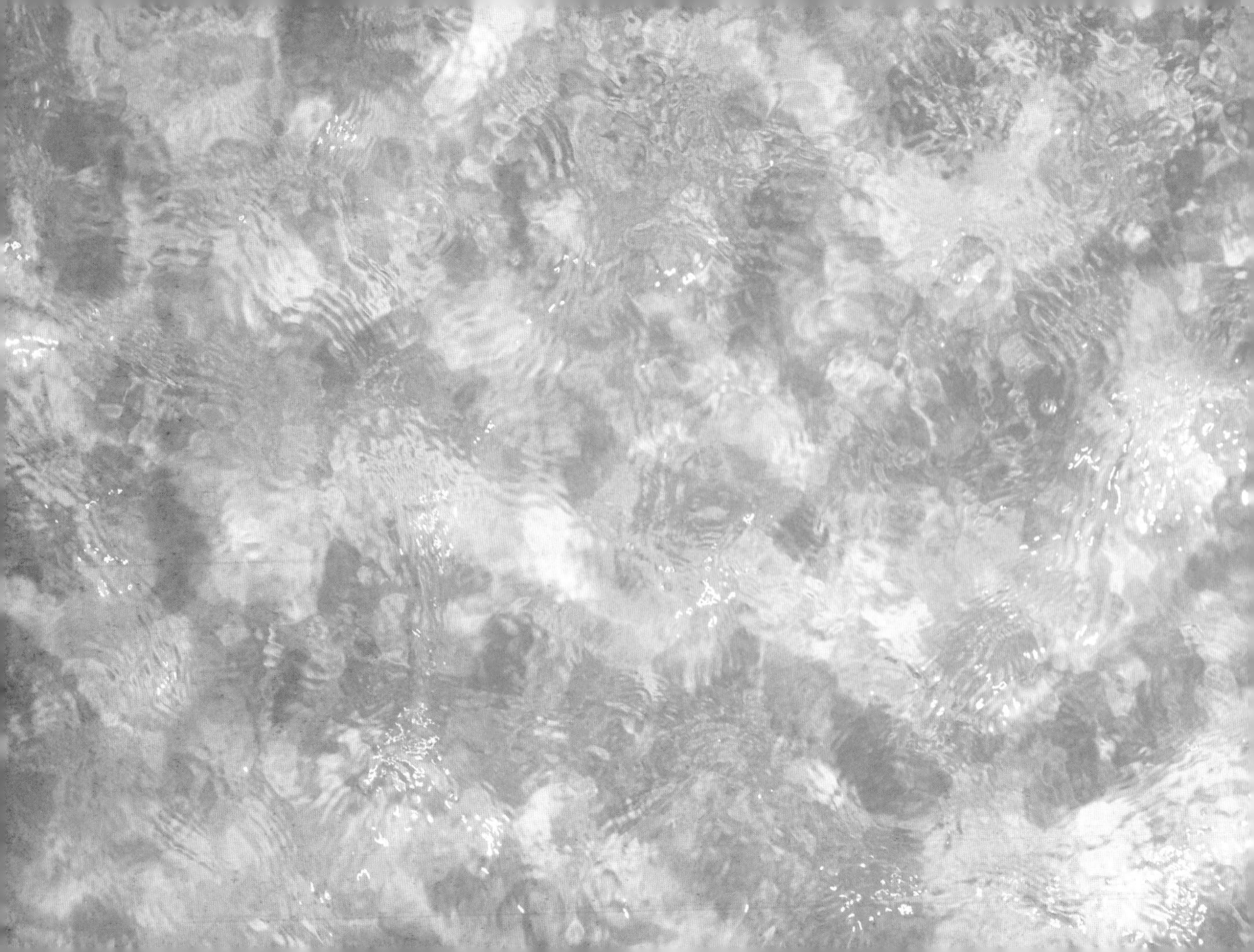

Close
Encounters
of the
Frog Kind

The Push-Pull Frog

Tom was good looking, fun and smart. There was just something about him that didn't click for me. I couldn't put my finger on it. I just wasn't interested. But he was! In a major way. And he wouldn't give up. He pursued me. And pursued me.

And, yes, he finally won me.

You know this guy. We *all* know this guy. He loves the chase. He pursues us, woos us and wows us with charm. We're not even sure that we want to go out with him. But he's so sweet, so persistent, so giving—we not only go out with him, we give in to him, and finally we *fall* for him.

Then, he pulls away! He starts being less giving, less available. He becomes distant. Then, in a flash—he's totally gone.

We don't understand. What went wrong? We had developed such a close relationship. We were an item.

The next month is miserable—and lonely. We miss him. We pine for him.

Finally, we let go of our pain and start dating again. We meet someone new. We're happy again. Then . . . he calls again.

It's simple. The Push-Pull Frog enjoys playing leapfrog with *your* heart. You're not available—he wants you. He gets you. He doesn't want you anymore. Then, as soon as he hears you're going with someone else . . . Guess what? He leaps back.

"I was such a fool," he says. "I miss you."

You're skeptical. But then he says the magic words: "I love you!"

What else can you do? You dump the new Joe and go back to Tom.

Surprise! He stomps on your heart and

splits again. Ladies, at the first sign of a Push-Pull frog, take my advice: Push-push him away.

Far away. So far away you can't even hear him "ribbet."

Toad on the Road

The only time he's in town is *your* time of the month!

Thwart-a-Wart: If his constant companion is his suitcase, send him packing.

75

The Tadpole

Oooh! He's a *hottie*—a real babe. He has this tight, hard body with cute little buns and power pecs. And more zip than the Energizer Bunny. He keeps going and going and going.

Stop. Put your brakes on!

It's okay if a guy is a *few* years younger than you are. But what if he's 10 years younger or 15 or—oops, could it be—20?

So, why not? Men have been dating (and marrying) younger women for centuries. Why not the other way around? I'll tell you *why not.* First of all, there's the embarrassment factor:

You're older than his mother. You look like his mother. People *presume* you're his mother. (Actually, you take *Feng Shui* with his mother.)

You not only have to buy him dinner, you have to cut it for him, too.

People mistake him for your little brother. Or they mistake him for your son. Or they mistake him for a gigolo. (Actually, he's a frogolo.)

On the street you run into your ex-boyfriend. It's humiliating. It turns out your tadpole and your ex-boyfriend's date went to their prom together—last year! She's 20 years younger than you, and three sizes smaller, too. Hey, you can always go home and take diet pills. (I tried that. I didn't eat less; I just ate faster.)

Secondly, there's the impractical factor: He wants children; you've already had them. Or, you want children; he's not ready. And how about: You want a child. He *is* one.

Of course, even though it may be both embarrassing and impractical, there may be some *teeny tiny* reasons to date a tadpole. After all, for some negatives, there are positives:

His parents look at you funny. His friends look at you funny. *Your* friends look at you funny. *But you have lots of sex.*

You and the tad have nothing to talk about. *But you don't have to talk during sex.*

You go to a video store to rent a movie. You want *Casablanca*. He wants *Dumb and Dumber*. (In fact, that's how you're starting to feel.) *But not when you're having sex.*

You want to play golf. He wants to play Nintendo. *But that night you play "Dirty Doctor."*

He wears braces. You wear dentures. *But when you kiss, sparks fly.*

For dinner, you want to go to a French bistro; he wants to go to Burger King. *But for dessert, you share his Whopper.*

He buys you a surprise for your birthday. You're hoping for jewelry. It's a PlayStation. *But he also buys you crotchless panties.* The panties don't fit you. *But they fit him!*

You go to each other's class reunions. His classmates are Christina Aguilera and Ricky Martin. Your classmates are dead. *But in bed he makes you feel alive.*

You want to go to an art gallery. He wants to go to Water Splash. *But that night he takes you to paradise.*

You're a guest at a charity ball. He's a busboy. *But he's also a dish!*

You catch yourself telling your friends, "Like wow. I met this way cool, like totally awesome dude!" *But in bed, you catch yourself yelling, "Oh God, Oh God, Oh God!"*

Which brings us to the statistics: Women reach their sexual peak at 35. Men reach their sexual peak at 18. So do the math and sum it up:

He has a great body + He has great stamina + He looks great naked + You have lots of

sex + You have frequent sex + You have great sex = S-E-X!

So why in the world would you *not* want to go out with The Tadpole? I'll tell you *why*:

Just as boys grow up to be men, tadpoles grow up to be frogs. Only faster. Remember, even though he's your boy toy, you'll be the toy that gets tossed!

So enjoy yourself for two weeks or two months of playful fun and sex, then end it and go hunting for a prince who will last forever!

The Frogtogenarian

So what if he had wrinkles, cataracts, and varicose veins?
I met him in Puerto Vallarta.
He took me to Puerto Viagra!

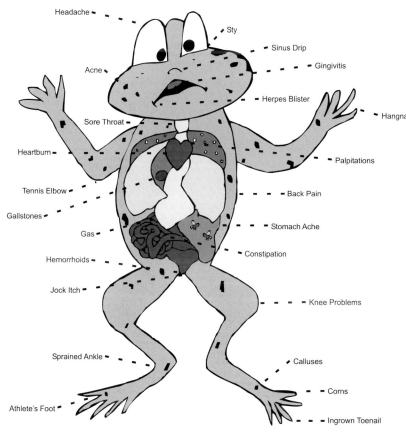

Headache

Sty

Sinus Drip

Gingivitis

Acne

Herpes Blister

Hangna

Sore Throat

Heartburn

Palpitations

Tennis Elbow

Back Pain

Gallstones

Gas

Stomach Ache

Hemorrhoids

Constipation

Jock Itch

Knee Problems

Sprained Ankle

Calluses

Corns

Athlete's Foot

Ingrown Toenail

Take Two Flies and Call Me in the Morning

If he always complains of aches and pains—your relationship needs dissecting.
Cut him out of your life!

Frognote: He doesn't need a girl-friend; he needs a paramedic!

The Groggy Froggy

He falls asleep. Not just at bedtime. He falls asleep in movies, in restaurants and at the mall.

Okay, once in a shoe store, several women actually *complimented* me on having found the *best possible* boyfriend. As I was trying on shoes, Ken was fast asleep on the chair.

"You're lucky he doesn't rush you," one shopper said.

Another woman piped in, "Yeah, my husband's always kvetching I take too long."

So while it may be okay at a shoe store, it doesn't work for me at other places. Like at a dinner party, an art opening, or during lovemaking. Unfortunately, Ken would fall asleep not *after* making love, but *during*.

The problem was that Ken would regularly get up at four in the morning, exercise, then go to work, work hard, come home, and *that's* when we'd see each other. Call me crazy but I didn't enjoy watching him sleep. It's just not my idea of a hot time.

And weekends weren't any different. No actually, I take that back. They *were* different. They were worse! He'd still get up at four, go mountain biking for five hours, then lift weights for two. By the time we met for dinner, he was like a narcoleptic on industrial strength Xanax.

One day I scored some hard-to-get tickets for a hot new play. Front row seats. I begged Ken, "Please set your alarm for later on Friday. Maybe instead of 4 a.m., you could get up at six? Or maybe seven?"

"No problem," he said.

I wasn't buying it. "It's supposed to be a

phenomenal show," I reiterated. "The tickets were expensive. I want you to enjoy it!"

"Don't worry, I'll get up at seven!"

"It stars *Faye Dunaway*!"

"Alright, I'll get up at *eight*!"

Friday came. Ken didn't change his alarm. He figured he could handle it all. He got up at four, exercised, went to work, worked hard. Left early to pick me up.

We went for a quick bite then headed to the theater.

It was opening night. The house was packed. And the buzz had been right. The play was magnificent. Mid first act, the two stars were immersed in a highly dramatic scene charged with emotion. Then, a moment of silence as Faye Dunaway choked back tears.

The air was thick with tension—the height of drama!

Suddenly, the mood was interrupted. By loud snores . . . emanating from the front row— from Ken, the sleeping giant.

I jabbed him. He awoke with a start. The audience gave us a collective shushhh!

Ken wanted to sleep. I wanted to die. It was time for me to take my show on the road.

Thwart-a-Wart: If he sleeps on opening night, it should be *closing night* for him.

81

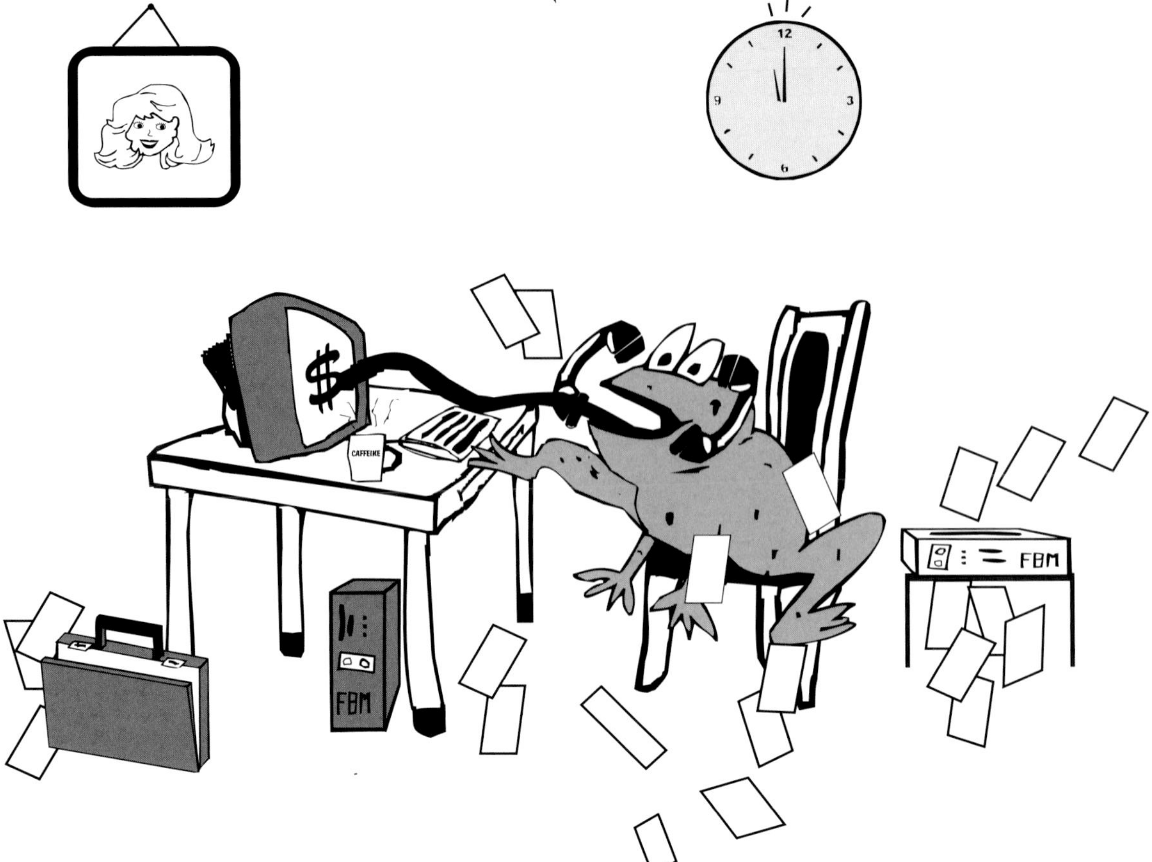
CAFFEINE
FBM
FBM

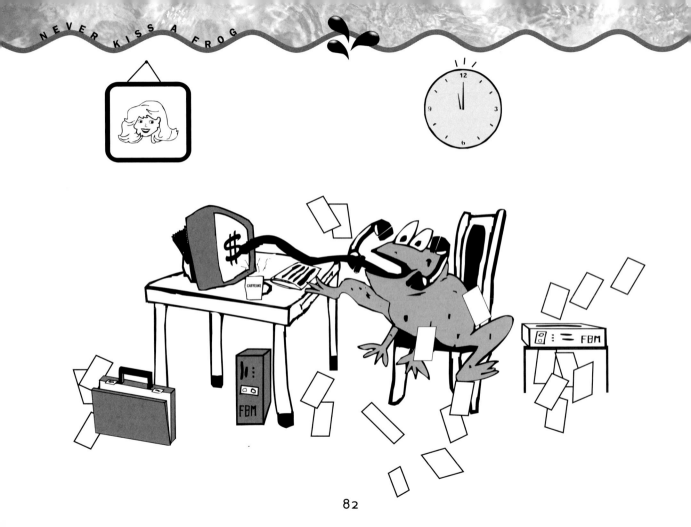

The All-Work-and-No-Play Frog

*W*e all know this one: a.k.a. The Workaholic Frog.

He's too busy.

He can't make dates.

He's late for dates.

He breaks dates

Often at the last minute.

Then, when you finally *do* get together, all he does is talk about his business. Or your "date" is at dinner with his business associates. Ooh—you get to listen in on the fascinating world of diesel oil truck stops!

Sometimes you get to go out on a *real* date—just the two of you. And he doesn't talk to you about business. Instead, he does his business by cell phone. It rings every two minutes. Following which, he has to make at least three or four calls to colleagues on their cell phones (who are out with *their* happy dates, of course). Don't you love technology?

Okay, so his ringing phone interrupts your dinner, the movie or your lovemaking. What's the big deal? I'll tell you. Whether it's a big deal, a mini-deal or a mega-deal, the deal on wheeler-dealers is: If you're not interested in being his *business* partner, you don't want this man for a *life* partner.

Thwart-a-Wart: If business consumes him every minute—when he goes home to bed, don't you be in it.

The All-Play-and-No-Work Frog

I live in Los Angeles where this is a common species. Morning, noon, and night, guys are going to the beach, tanning, surfing, skateboarding and sitting at coffeehouses or sidewalk cafes. They're always playing, loafing, relaxing or simply hanging out. They never seem to work.

Okay, so maybe a few of these guys have a pension or a rich aunt or live off their investments. Just beware of the ones who want to live off you.

Early Warting Signs

1. Instead of a sign: "Will Work for Food," he carries a sign: "Will Date for Food."

Ribbet Snippet

Whether he's a beach bum, a ski bum, or a tennis bum—this guy is a *bum deal* for you.

84

2. He tells you he's madly in love and he wants to move in right away. What he doesn't tell you is that he needs a place to stay!

3. He's at Starbucks 24/7. But he doesn't drink coffee. He brings his own teabag—and collects *their* sugar packets.

4. He always picks you up for dates on roller blades, even when you're not going blading.

5. Homeless people on the street know him by name. When he walks by, they hand *him* money.

6. He knows the location of every Happy Hour in town. And what free hors d'oeuvres are served on which days.

7. He says he's on an "extended" vacation. What he means is he's *permanently unemployed.*

8. The only thing he's ever worked at is getting a tan. Even then, he complains about the hours.

Gamblers Frognonymous

If your joker plays too much poker—deal him out!

Surfing the Webbed Feet

*A*h, love on the Internet! It's fantastic: a whole world of men at your fingertips. You can meet someone who lives across the street or across the continent. And it works! I actually know women who met their husbands over the web. (I also know women who met other women's husbands over the web.)

As for me, I've logged onto Kissme.com, Matchmaker.com, Lastchance.com, Desperatetomarry.org, and Oldmaids-R-Us.com.

I met Josh on If-I-Don't-Meet-Someone-Soon-I'll-Kill-Myself.com. I was immediately taken with his screen name: Can Go All Night. This was the man for me!

I e-mailed him my photo. It was love at first byte. He started sending me the most incredibly romantic and poetic e-mails. Every night I'd come home and find some divine electronic missive from my soon-to-be prince. We became cyber soul mates.

Finally, after weeks of Internet dialog, we graduated to the phone. Our conversation was brief. "Let's meet."

We had drinks at a local nightspot. Almost immediately, I could feel the electricity. But I also felt *static*. (My brain was trying to send a

message to the rest of my body: "Wart Alert, Wart Alert!" But unfortunately, it never reached my inner thighs, which for some strange reason were quivering and tingling.)

What the hell? We left the bar and, when we got to my apartment, I invited him in. He was tremendously excited.

But not for the reason I expected.

Once inside, instead of playing with my tank top, he started playing with my desktop! I tried to push him away but he wouldn't take no for an answer. And he knew all the right buttons to push. My Gateway opened right up to him.

In an instant, he started probing and pounding my waiting keypad. His hand cupped my mouse. Then he unzipped my zip drive. A power surge went through my parallel port. I yelled, "Stop. Please. Stop!" But Josh kept going. Sending his stream of data through my firewall. His eyes looked deep into my monitor.

He moaned with delight as he entered chat room after chat room.

There was the Married-Women-Who-Want-to-Sleep-with-Albino-Mutants Chat Room, the Short-Men-with-Napoleon-Complexes-Who-Seem-Taller-on-the-Computer Chat Room and The-Body-Piercing-Love-to-Suffer-Hate-Myself Chat Room.

Josh was an equal-opportunity cyber-frog. He went into gay men chat rooms and lesbian chat rooms, bisexual and transsexual chat rooms, even the Hermaphrodites-Go-Both-Ways Chat Room. He loved to role-play. On the web, he could be anyone to anybody. (How well I knew—he had been a prince to me!)

"Please. You have to leave," I begged. "I'm about to crash."

"Just a little longer," he implored. It was already 3:00 a.m.

"Josh, when you said you could go all

night, I thought you meant something else."

"Okay, I'll get off in a minute," he said, inserting his floppy disk into my drive. "And don't worry, I won't give you a virus. I've got protection!"

That was it. I grabbed his floppy, zipped his drive, and pushed him away from my Gateway. Then I shoved him out the door.

I looked at my poor violated Gateway. It needed a cold shower.

The next night, I got a long e-mail from Josh. I didn't read it. Instead, I forwarded it to Badfirstdates.com.

The moral of this story, ladies? When you're surfing the web, watch out for frog bytes.

Thwart-a-Wart: Next time he logs on—delete his hard drive. Re-boot. Re-boot. Re-boot!

Frog-in-the-Box

He pops up every now and then.
Then disappears again.
Say, "So long, Jack!"

section six

Hoppily Ever After

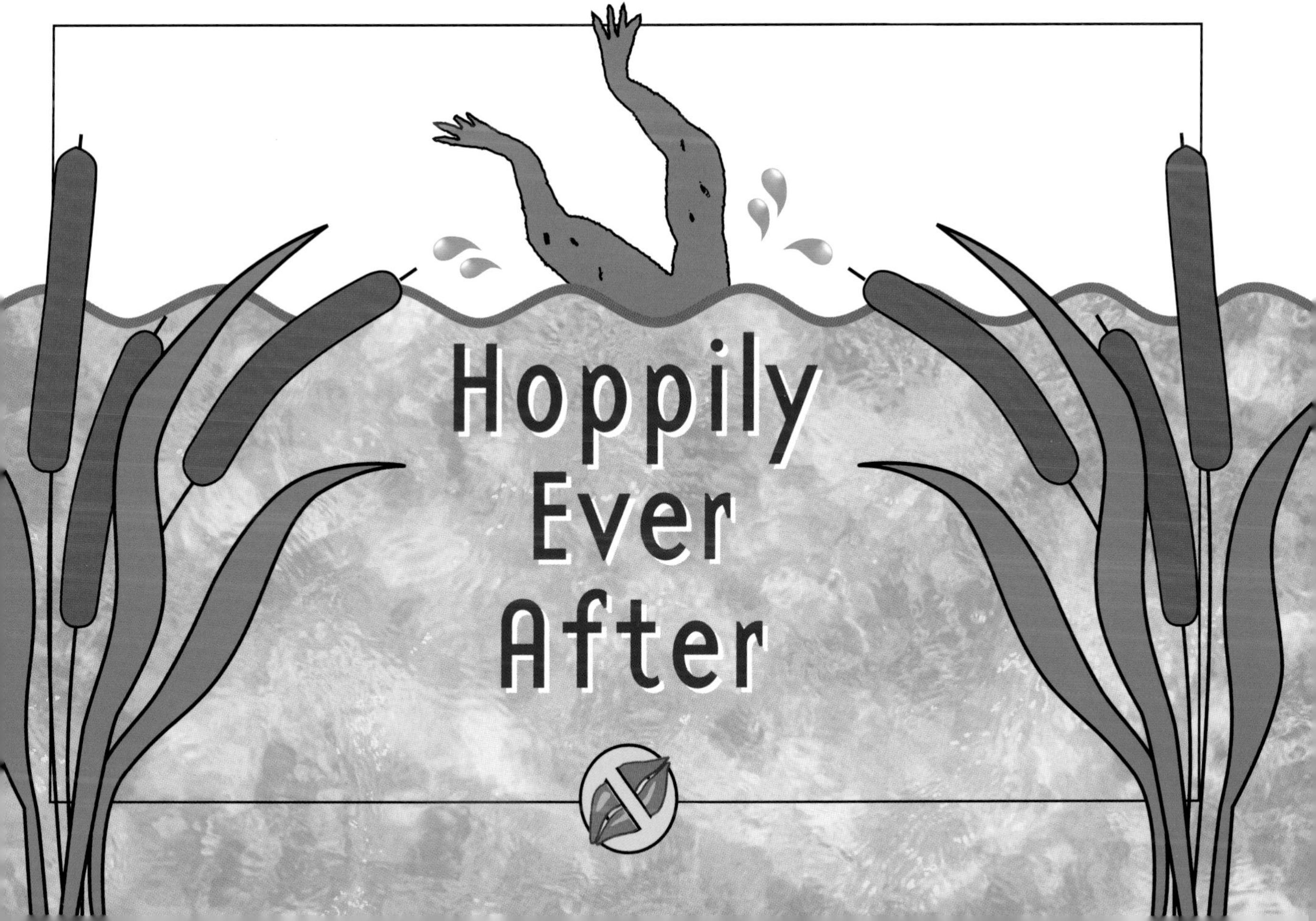

The Frog Who Would Be Prince

So here I am still trudging through the swamp when suddenly I spot him. His lips are all puckered up and ready to go. He stares straight at me and gazes deep into my eyes. "Kiss me!" he says.

I hesitate. After all, I'm wiser now.

"C'mon, Princess," he cajoles, "I'm not like the others. I really am a prince!"

What do I do?

And if you meet this frog—what should *you* do?

Girls, please! You've just read a whole book about how a frog *does not, will not* and *cannot* turn into a prince. A frog is a frog is a frog. That's the absolute truth. Except for one little thing: Just as one person's junk can be another person's treasure, one woman's frog can be another woman's prince.

So what am I saying here? That women should trade frogs the way kids trade Pokemon Cards? Not exactly. I'm not suggesting that if you know an outright jerk-sonofabitch-turkey-slimeball-drip, you should pass him on to Cousin Jenny. Unless of course it's Cousin Jenny who screwed you out of your Aunt Sophie's inheritance.

However, if you are dating a charming man with four dogs and three cats but the slightest trace of pet dander sends you into anaphylactic shock, this man is not for you. On the other hand, he's perfect for a girl who majored in animal husbandry!

And what if your newest date goes sailing every weekend but you get seasick in a bathtub? My advice is to abandon ship and find a landlubber. However, if you have a friend who kayaks, she might appreciate an introduction to the captain you threw overboard.

Likewise, if you're involved with a sweet, loving soul who *bores* you, don't waste time hoping he'll get a personality transplant. Instead, set him up with one of your boring co-workers. Together, they might make it down the aisle and produce some boring children. And tell her to send *you* that handsome, smart, successful guy whose jokes go way over her head. You never know . . . Her frog might just turn into *your* prince.

When You Wish Upon a Frog

Someday my prince will come. Sounds great, doesn't it? But how in the world do I find him? And how will you find yours?

Not by wishing, I can assure you. No. There's only one way, girls: *Keep looking!* I know I'm sure going to!

That's right. I'm not giving up.

What? You thought, because I wrote this Frog Bible, that I hate men? No way! I don't even dislike men. I *love* men. I love how they look; I love how they feel; I love how they smell. (Okay, not *always* how they smell.)

What's more, I love their beards and their stubble, their hairy arms and their hairy legs and their hairy chests, and I'll even forgive a hairy back, now and then. I love all—well, most—of the ways that men are different from me. And I hunger for the man who will make my heart soar.

Who knows where we'll meet? At a party? In a bar? In a restaurant? Or a nursing home? God knows, I hope I don't have to wait that long.

How will I know it's *him*? He'll look across the room at me and I'll get butterflies. He'll take my hand, and my knees will go weak. And when he takes me in his arms and kisses me, I'll melt. (If this is too sappy, you have my permission to gag. But hey, I'm a romantic!)

We'll spend our days laughing and our nights making love. We'll whisper sweet nothings and shout obscene somethings. And then, we'll ooh and ah, and huff and puff, and moan and groan. And, if necessary, we'll adjust our pacemakers!

You see, I want romance. I want passion. I want love. And I want to walk down that aisle! And I believe it's not over 'til it's over. The proverbial fat lady hasn't sung.

In fact, someone is going to sing. Oh yeah, there's going to be music. You would hear it now except my publishers wouldn't approve the cost of a microchip that would play Elvis singing "Love Me Tender." And they wouldn't cough up for virtual-reality glasses, either. So just *pretend* you have on a pair of really cool surround-sound, virtual-reality goggles. Now lean back and watch as the music builds and images pop up all around you. It's the final scene of a wonderful new movie—my movie.

My Big Fat Green Wedding

FADE IN: AN ELEGANT BALLROOM

Exquisitely dressed men and women are dancing. The double doors at the front of the room swing open.

I enter, looking demure yet hot in a classy, long velvet skirt and jacket. I glide through the crowd.

Suddenly, across the dance floor, a suave, handsome, Tom Cruise type stares at me. Everyone else in the room disappears. The music swells. He races toward me . . . lifts me and twirls me around.

DISSOLVE TO:

An instant replay of my favorite fairytales—*Cinderella, Snow White* and *Sleeping Beauty*—the scenes where each damsel rides off with her prince.

CUT BACK TO: THE ELEGANT BALLROOM

The man carries me up the marble staircase. Suddenly, there's a flash of light—it's my Fairy Frogmother! She waves her magic wand. My skirt and jacket turn into a beautiful wedding gown—by Armani.

It's my wedding day! The ballroom magically morphs into a Wedding Hall. Everybody is here. All the fairytale people: Grumpy, Sneezy and Dopey and the other dwarfs, and all my frogs, dressed in tuxes, of course. You can

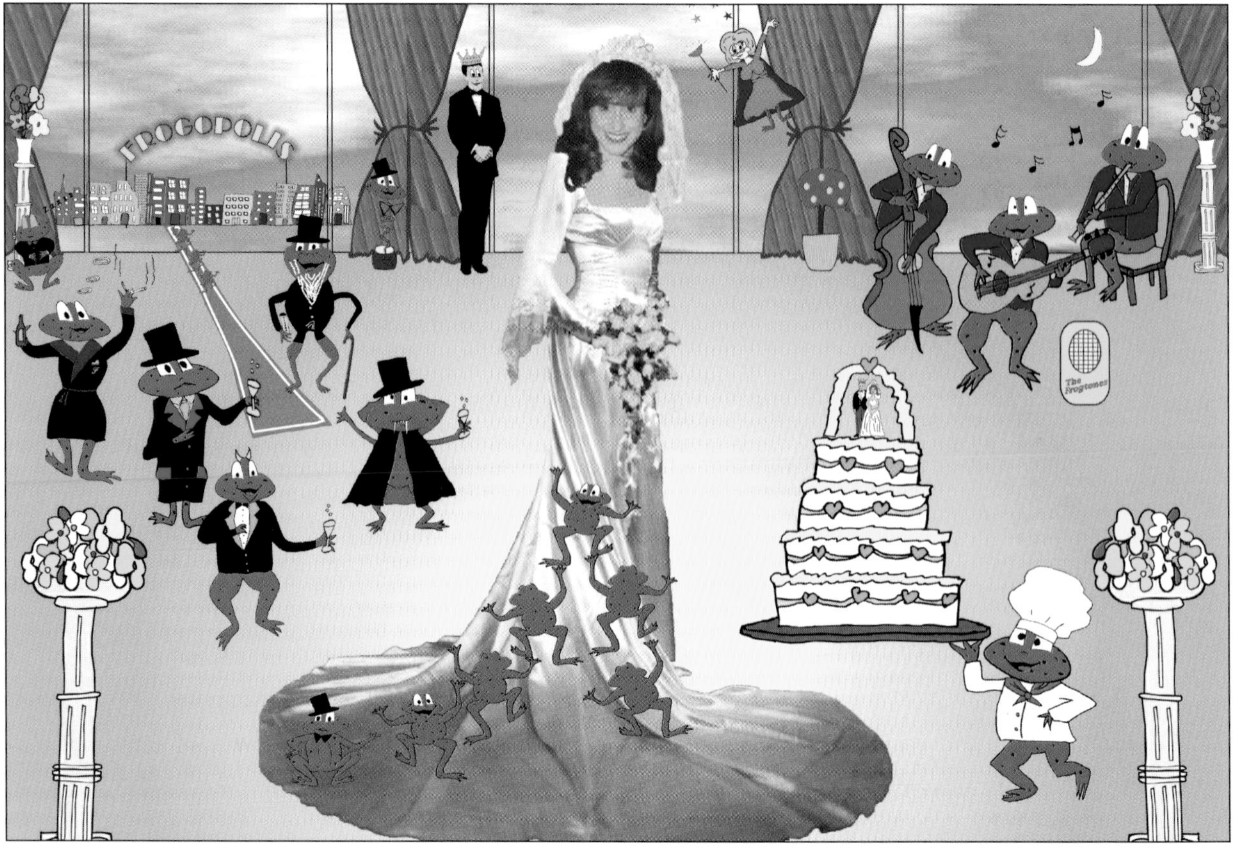
FROGOPOLIS
The Frogtones

see The Tadpole, Sir Frogalot and The Horny Toad (hitting on my best friend). And there's the mean stepmother and the ugly stepsisters (hey, *everyone's* invited), all my aunts and uncles who had given up hope, and my mom and dad who wanted this day even more than I did!

I start walking down the aisle. I look *phenomenal*. The music swells. Then a vocalist steps forward. It's Barbara Streisand!

That's right—Streisand. She sings "Evergreen." Hey, she insisted. She knew it was going to be the event of the 21st century. All the frogs I ever dated watch with envy. I don't even care if they ribbet as I walk by. I reach the altar. The music stops. My groom takes my hand. The rabbi asks me, "Do you take this man?" My mother screams out, "SHE DOES!"

My new husband and I embrace. It's a long, idyllic kiss.

CUT TO: THE RECEPTION

We have Chinese food. And Italian. And Thai-Hungarian Fusion. (I told you it was going to be *the* event.) Aretha Franklin heads up the band. They play the hottest blues you've ever heard. I dance with my husband all night. It's glorious and raucous.

And later, we head off to our honeymoon suite. Our legs hungrily entwine and our quivering loins thrust toward each other like giant pulsating magnets coming together and exploding in a burst of exquisite ecstasy. Then we get out of the elevator.

CUT TO: THE HONEYMOON SUITE

We go into our suite and leap onto the heart-shaped bed, where we make mad, passionate love for days. Now, this is the part where you have to take off your goggles. This part is private—just for me and my prince.

Beyond the Pond

The point is, I still believe. I still have hopes and dreams. And I'm still out there looking, whether I'm working out at the gym or walking down the street, browsing the personals or surfing the Internet, whether I'm attending an opera in my silk Versace or taking out the garbage in my rubber flip-flops.

I don't know where I'll find him or where he'll find me. But one thing is for sure. I still believe in those romantic fairytales I read as a little girl. I still believe in Happily Ever After. And in my heart, I still believe that *SOMEDAY MY PRINCE WILL COME!*

And, my dear friends, so will *yours.*

Just remember this: *You can't find a prince if you're busy kissing frogs!*

Congratulations!

By reading this book, you have become an honorary member of *Frogaholics Anonymous,* a 12-leap program. There's also *Froganon*, for friends of Frogaholics. So cut out the emblem below and display it proudly—or give it to a needy girlfriend. And you're all invited to visit me at www.neverkissafrog.com

NEVER KISS A FROG